SPRINGBOARD TO SUCCESS
COMMUNICATION STRATEGIES FOR THE CLASSROOM AND BEYOND

PATRICIA SKILLMAN

CHEIRON MCMAHILL

PRENTICE HALL REGENTS
A VIACOM COMPANY

Editorial Director: *Arley Gray*
Manager of Development Services: *Louisa B. Hellegers*
Development Editor: *Lida Baker*

Director of Production: *Aliza Greenblatt*
Editorial Production / Design Manager: *Dominick Mosco*
Electronic production and interior page design: *D. Andrew Gitzy*

Production Coordinator: *Ray Keating*
Art Director: *Merle Krumper*
Cover Designer: *Jayne Conte*

Printed in the United States of America

10   9   8   7   6   5   4   3

ISBN 0-205-15613-4

Prentice Hall International (UK) Limited, *London*
Prentice Hall of Australia Pty. Limited, *Sydney*
Prentice Hall Canada, Inc., *Toronto*
Prentice Hall Hispanoamericana, S.A., *Mexico*
Prentice Hall Of India Private Limited, *New Delhi*
Prentice Hall of Japan, Inc., *Tokyo*
Simon & Schuster Asia Pte. Ltd., *Singapore*
Editora Prentice Hall do Brasil, Ltda., *Rio de Janeiro*

TABLE OF CONTENTS

Chapter Four
Negotiating with Instructors **Page 67**

Chapter Topics
- ask about course requirements and instructor policies
- make appointments with instructors
- excuse yourself for tardiness, absences, or late or missed work
- ask about your grade in a class
- request special arrangements

Follow Up Activities
- discuss and find solutions for problems with instructors
- discuss cheating and plagiarizing
- talk to your instructor privately
- get advice about communicating with instructors
- give a short presentation about a "favorite" teacher
- interview someone about their favorite teacher

Chapter Five
Giving a Demonstration **Page 99**

Chapter Topics
- give a clear, interesting explanation on how to do something
- introduce and give background information for a demonstration
- clearly communicate what you want your audience to do, and not do
- invite participation from your audience
- give encouragement

Follow Up Activities
- give a detailed demonstration on how to do something in your culture
- learn about and share American culture

Chapter Six
Giving Short Speeches **Page 117**

Chapter Topics
- organize a speech
- speak so that you are understood
- use appropriate body language
- coach you classmates

Follow Up Activities
- pausing and stressing key words
- making note cards
- give a short speech
- give a speech based on an out-of-class interview
- observe a speech

Chapter Twelve
Preparing for Future Challenges

Chapter Topics
- talk about your plans for the future
- state your concerns
- locate school support systems
- ask for help
- manage your time
- take lecture notes
- study for tests

Follow Up Activities
- listen to a lecture on how to take lecture notes
- inquire about student services at a nearby college
- report on your efforts to improve your study habits and manage your time better
- find out about academic policies and procedures

Appendix One
Script and Answer Keys

Appendix Two
Feedback Forms (Tear-out forms)

Chapter Organization

Rhythm Practices

These are chants that help students with vocabulary, pronunciation, and intonation through rhythm and repetition.

Model Conversations

These conversation introduce the chapter or section theme and target expressions and skills in context.

Preview Questions

These questions elicit the prior experiences of students in order to predict the section's content and preview vocabulary.

Overviews

These are charts that assist students in identifying the target structures for that section and classifying expressions according to function or situation.

Practices

These are controlled or semi-controlled pair and group exercises for the practice of Overview expressions.

Review of Overview Expressions

These are cloze exercises to check students' acquisition of target expressions before moving on to application activities.

Follow Up

These are more extensive individual, pair, and group projects that require students to apply expressions and skills to accomplish a personalized task in or out of class.

TO THE INSTRUCTOR

For your quick reference, here is a brief overview of *Springboard to Success* and how to use it. More detailed information on teaching each chapter and on using this textbook as a whole can be found in the separate Instructor's Manual. There is also a cassette tape available from the publisher of the Model Conversations and Rhythm Practices for each chapter.

I. *Springboard to Success: Communication Strategies for the Classroom and Beyond*

Purpose

This textbook is aimed at helping intermediate students to participate and speak more effectively in the immediate ESL classroom, and also at giving them skills and knowledge to transfer to their academic classes or future jobs. It takes a thoroughly hands-on approach, requiring students to get to know each other, work together smoothly, and explore their own cultures and American culture. The result is a dynamic class where students spend the majority of time listening to each other, thinking, and expressing themselves.

Intended Students

This text was written for intermediate students of ESL who need or will need to use English for academic or professional purposes. They could be students in the upper levels of an intensive English program, or students already attending American colleges and universities but completing some ESL or orientation classes. They could also be students in foreign countries preparing to study in the U.S. or beginning to take classes at American branch campuses. This textbook is also helpful in the immediate goal of helping students adjust to the teaching style of an instructor from an American cultural background and the expectations of their ESL program, whether they are going on to academic content classes or not.

The Need for *Springboard to Success*

Intermediate students can't wait until they get to advanced oral communication classes to understand the how, when, and why of speaking in American academic classes. Students need such instruction as soon as they join an American style classroom, which is often the ESL class.

Students also need to explore and confirm how their ability to communicate in the classroom and on the campus fits in with their success. But even when schools offer orientation classes and study skills labs to this end, students typically need more time and guidance in testing out the information they are given.

Springboard to Success uses familiar and clear language and examples to integrate instruction in academic speaking with the content of American academic expectations and study skills. *Springboard to Success* helps the intermediate student simultaneously develop knowledge, strategies, and speaking skills for academic achievement.

II. Chapter Organization

Each chapter progresses from short, controlled activities to open-ended, large projects, as you can see in the outline on page vi (see **VI. General Teaching Suggestions**, for more description and instructions on how to teach each section).

You can adjust the material to your students' level(s) by emphasizing the first half of each chapter (from "Rhythm Practice" to "Review of Overview Sections") with lower level classes, and the latter half of each chapter ("Follow Up") with higher level students.

We tried to provide "more-than-enough" examples and activities to meet each chapter's instructional goals, so that you would have to do little modifying or supplementing. Especially, there are many choices given for extension activities in the Follow Up sections and you should choose only the one(s) best for your class.

Finally, you do not have to wait until the end of the chapter to start Follow Up activities. You can begin them before finishing the Practices or as you see fit in order to complete them conveniently within your class schedule.

III. Sequencing

The chapters are in the order we found usually best fits the flow of the class and the progress of the students, starting, for example, with Chapter 1 and getting to know classmates and the teacher, and ending with Chapter 12 and making concrete preparations for academic subject classes. But in fact, you can choose any order that meets your and your students' interests and goals. Although many chapters relate to and reinforce what is taught in other chapters, you can pick and choose and even go back and forth as needed between several chapters depending on what you need at that time.

Here are some suggestions for varying the sequence of the chapters:

Chapters that make effective openers for a course:

• Learning from Your Classmates (Chapter One)

• Giving a Demonstration (Chapter Five)

• Discussing in Small Groups (Chapter Seven)

Chapters that make effective finales for a course:

• Planning and Performing a Role Play (Chapter Three)

• Giving Short Speeches (Chapter Six)

• Arguing Your Point (Chapter Ten)

Chapters that work well mid-term:

• Negotiating with Instructors (Chapter Four)

• Getting Help at the Library (Chapter Nine)

The Table of Contents on pages i–v gives a detailed overview of each chapter for your reference.

IV. Instructional time

Each chapter varies in length, but it takes an average of five to eight hours in class and two to four hours of homework to complete a chapter, including doing one Follow-Up activity. Again, this will vary depending on how much you want to emphasize the target structures, skills, and goals of that particular chapter, as well as on the level of the students. For example, instructors often choose to repeat an application activity once the skill has been learned; i.e., do a second debate, a more formal discussion, a speech that includes library research, and so on.

V. Suggestions for testing and evaluation

1. cloze tests

You can make up cloze tests similar to the "Review of Overview Expressions" to test acquisition of the target expressions; some examples are given in the teaching notes for each chapter in the instructor's manual.

2. listening comprehension tests

While the emphasis of this text is on speaking, the end result is that students' listening comprehension also improves. You can test this by using the cassette tape of the Model Conversation that is available from the publisher, or making a recording of a similar conversation yourself. You can then create either short answer questions (in small classes) or multiple choice questions (in large classes) about the content or usage.

3. oral evaluation

Many forms and suggestions are given for evaluating the students oral work, both in the back of the students' books and in the teaching notes in the Instructors' Manual, and a numerical or letter grade can be assigned at the same time.

4. portfolio assessment

In smaller classes, you can stress the goals of active and responsible learning by having students keep a portfolio of all their work in the class, including oral journal cassette tapes, any videotapes, notes from interviews, scripts of presentations, written reports, and evaluation forms filled out by the student, their peers, and you. Students' and your evaluation of this portfolio can then be used to determine all or a portion of a grade in the class. You can involve students even more by going over their portfolios with them in a final private conference.

Sample evaluation guidelines and forms for portfolio assessment can be found in the Instructor's Manual.

VI. General teaching suggestions

The purpose of activities common to all chapters and brief suggestions for teaching them are given below. For more detailed suggestions on Follow Up activities and adapting the activities to multilevel or large classes, please see the Instructor's Manual.

Rhythm Practice

These are chants that help students remember the vocabulary, pronunciation, and intonation patterns of some of the target expressions of the entire chapter through rhythm and repetition. A model tape of the chants is available through the publisher.

1. Explain the context of the chant briefly.

2. Have students just listen several times to you or the tape.

3. Have students keep time with the rhythm by clapping their hands or tapping their desks.

4. Divide the class in half; have one side repeat A's part after you and the other side, B's; then reverse.

5. Practice slowly a couple times, then more quickly.

6. Have students practice several times in pairs, adding any gestures that seem appropriate; circulate and help students at this time.

7. Ask two or three of the pairs to do the chant in front of the class.

Model Conversation

This conversation or conversations introduce the chapter or section theme and target expressions and skills in a context, provide practice in listening comprehension and pronunciation, and give the class a chance to discuss usage and social appropriateness.

1. Explain the context.

2. Let students read it silently.

3. Read it out loud several times, or play the tape available from the publisher.

4. Have students read it in pairs or small groups, changing parts each time.

5. Have students answer the questions first with a partner, then call on students to answer in front of the class; put answers up on board. (The questions can also be assigned ahead of time as homework).

6. Expand on and clarify answers.

Preview Questions

These questions elicit the prior experiences of students that are relevant to that segment of the chapter, encourage students to predict the section's content, and preview vocabulary.

1. Go over questions first, rephrasing and giving examples.

2. Have students interview each other using the questions in pairs or small groups (the questions can also be assigned as homework).

3. Call on two or three students for each question; compare and expand on their answers.

Overview

This is a chart that assists students in identifying the target structures for that section and classifying expressions according to function or situation. It provides a range of alternatives to suit students' level and preference and encourages students to become aware of and share other similar expressions they know or hear. It can also be used to provide practice in pronunciation and intonation, and as a handy reference for students as they work on practices and Follow Up activities.

1. Read out loud; students listen.

2. While reading, explain vocabulary and any nuances such as formality or informality.

3. Also while reading, have students circle stressed (focus) words and draw lines between words to indicate reductions and linking (see Instructor's Manual for examples).

4. Read out loud; students repeat.

5. Students find and underline expressions from the Overview in the Model Conversation.

6. Students try to find other expressions as homework.

7. Refer students back to Overview during Practices.

Practices

These are controlled or semi-controlled pair and group exercises for the practice of overview expressions. They give students opportunities to ask questions and clarify meaning, and provide lots of contextualized, short examples of usage.

1. Model one of the exchanges with a student.

2. Many of the practices are gap activities where two students must obtain missing information from each other. After students find a partner, tell them to be either "Student A" or "Student B" and to look only at their own page. The first few times you do these exercises, you will have to model this clearly, get students to move their chairs and books so the other students can't see, and check to make sure they are not copying the missing information from the other students' page.

3. Ask two students to try one exchange or begin a practice in front of the class to make sure everyone understands how to do it.

4. Coach those two students to look up from the book and make eye contact with each other while they are doing the exercise, and reinforce this as you check on other pairs later.

5. Tell students to use expressions from the Overview.

6. Circulate quickly throughout the class to clarify misunderstandings.

7. Ask students who finish early to change parts and do it again, or to prepare to role-play one exchange or part of a practice in front of the class.

Review of Overview Expressions

This is a cloze exercise to check students' acquisition of target expressions before moving on to application activities. They also serve to show again how all the expressions and skills come together in a context, and to review intonation and pronunciation. They can be used as review before a similar cloze test if you desire.

1. Have students work alone for five minutes, filling in the blanks and changing the information whenever possible to be about themselves.

2. Ask them to check answers with a partner.

3. Let them look back at the Overviews to check answers.

4. Have students read the conversations out loud in pairs.

5. Ask students to close their books and reconstruct and role-play the situation from memory.

6. Ask one or two students to present their role-play to the class.

Follow Up

These are more extensive individual, pair, and group projects that require students to apply expressions and skills to accomplish a personalized task in or out of class. They allow students to more deeply internalize expressions and skills, gain confidence in their ability to negotiate tasks independently, and experience firsthand the usefulness of what they have been learning. Some Follow Up activities are to be done in class, such as role-plays, presentations, games, discussions, and self-evaluation of work on the whole chapter. Others are to be done outside class, such as interviews, oral journals (reports that are recorded and turned in on cassette tape), field trips, observations, library research, and information gathering by phone.

1. Decide which of the Follow Up activities you'll do. If students haven't done that type of activity before, model it for them when first beginning the chapter. This gives students a clear idea of what they are working toward as they progress through the chapter. This means that the first time you do a Follow Up activity, you may need to create your own simple examples or visual aids; if the activity requires a pair or group presentation, you can demonstrate it with especially proficient students. Then, when students do the activity, videotape their presentations and save their materials to use as examples in the future.

2. For out-of-class activities such as observations and interviews, use your judgment about calling or visiting individuals, offices and facilities ahead of time to explain the purpose of the activity and ascertain their willingness and ability to provide information to students.

3. Whenever possible have students present or perform especially creative or culturally informative activities for community groups to promote contact and cultural exchange. Examples of possible venues are elementary schools, senior centers, and college classes studying a foreign language or region, anthropology, cross-cultural communication, and so on.

4. Follow Up activities can also be selected for oral testing and grading as is needed or desired. Feedback forms are provided as examples in the Instructor's Manual. Evaluation items can be given numerical scores in order to assign grades.

Appendix 1: Scripts and Answer Keys

These are scripts of teacher lectures, game cards, and answers to quizzes for students to use to check their answers. Although they are also for your reference, they were included here in the student book in case you do not have the instructor's manual.

Appendix 2: Feedback Forms

These forms assist students in systematically evaluating and improving their own and peers' work on specific tasks. They can be torn out and given to peers or the instructor.

1. Model filling in the form for students to make sure they understand how to use them (it can be effective to do this using an OHP).

2. Ask students to turn in the forms to you for your information and comments.

3. Consider grading or giving points to the person doing the peer feedback or self-evaluation to encourage them to put extra thought and detail into it.

4. Try to pair up students who get along well for peer feedback.

CHAPTER ONE

LEARNING FROM YOUR CLASSMATES

In this chapter, you will learn how to:

- introduce yourself
- work with a partner on class activities
- ask "delicate" questions politely
- discuss cultural differences and stereotypes

RHYTHM PRACTICE

In this chant, you will practice the pronunciation of vocabulary and expressions you need to introduce yourself.

Directions

1. Listen to the example chant. Then listen to your teacher introduce him or herself.
2. Repeat after your teacher.
3. Introduce yourself to the class. Everybody reads the chorus together.

Self-introduction:

Hi!

I'm (*first name, family name*)

From (*hometown, country*)

It's so NICE to meet ALL of you

I LIKE (*something*)

I HATE (*something*)

Now, tell ME a little about YOU.

Class chorus:

Hi (*first name*), who LIKES (. . .), but HATES (. . .)

(*continue for each person already introduced*)

HI (*first name*), who LIKES (. . .), but HATES (. . .)

HI (*first name*), who LIKES (. . .), but HATES (. . .)

It's nice to meet YOU, TOO.

Example

Sami: Hi!
I'm (SAmi al WARah)
From (CAIro, Egypt)
It's so NICE to meet ALL of you
I LIKE (to COOK)
I HATE (to CLEAN)
Now, tell ME a little about YOU.

Class chorus: HI Sami, who LIKES to COOK, but HATES to CLEAN
It's nice to meet YOU, TOO.

Ricardo: HI!
I'm (RiCARdo PeREZ)
From (São PAUlo, BraZIL)
It's so NICE to meet ALL of you
I LIKE (to DANCE)
I HATE (PoTAtoes)
Now, tell ME a little about YOU.

Class chorus: HI RiCARdo, who LIKES to DANCE, but HATES poTAtoes
HI SAmi, who LIKES to COOK, but HATES to CLEAN

(continue with names of others already introduced)

It's nice to meet YOU, TOO.

MODEL CONVERSATION

1. Read the conversation silently.
2. Listen to the conversation.
3. Read it out loud twice with a classmate, changing roles each time.
4. Answer the questions that follow.

(Two students are introducing themselves in class. The teacher has told them to find a partner to check the homework.)

Sami: Hi, do you have a partner?

Ricardo: No, let's work together. My name is Ricardo Perez. Please call me Ricardo.

Sami: It's nice to meet you, Ricardo. I'm Sami al Warah. I'm from Egypt. Where are you from?

Ricardo: I'm from São Paulo, which is in the southeast of Brazil. Where are you from in Egypt?

Sami: I'm from Cairo. (*pause*) So, do you speak Spanish?

Ricardo: I can understand a little, but actually we speak Portuguese in Brazil.

Sami: Oh, that's right. I'm afraid I don't know much about Brazil, but I just love Brazilian music.

Ricardo: Yeah, I'd give anything to hear some right now.

Sami: How long have you been in the States?

Ricardo: About a year. I'm trying to raise my TOEFL score, then I'm planning to enter a community college.

Sami: That's great. Good luck!

Ricardo: Thanks. How about you?

Sami: I'm majoring in chemistry. I'm here as an exchange student for a year.

Ricardo: Well, it's really nice to meet someone from Egypt. (*pause*) I hope you don't mind my asking, but do women have to wear veils in your country?

Sami:	There are some Egyptian women who wear veils, but it's not required. You must be thinking of a different country.
Ricardo:	I guess you're right. Well, we're supposed to check the homework. Are you ready?
Sami:	Sure. You go first.
Ricardo:	All right. I said "no" to number 1.
Sami:	Me, too.
Ricardo:	Your turn. What did you put for number 2?
Sami:	I put "sometimes, but it depends on the situation."
Ricardo:	Hmm, that's interesting. Why did you say that?

Questions on the Model Conversation:

1. How does Sami start the conversation with Ricardo?

2. What expressions do Sami and Ricardo use to introduce themselves?

3. People don't speak Spanish in Brazil, they speak Portuguese. How does Ricardo tell this to Sami gently?

4. How does Sami say he is sorry for thinking Brazilians speak Spanish?

5. When Ricardo asks about women wearing veils in Egypt, what polite expression does he use?

6. Why does Ricardo try to ask politely about veils? religion

7. Most women don't wear veils in Egypt —how does Sami tell this to Ricardo gently?

Section 1: Introducing Yourself

Preview Questions

1. In your country, what gestures or body language do people use to introduce themselves?

2. What do you tell people about yourself when you first meet?

3. What do you ask about them?

4. How are American self-introductions different from or similar to those in your native country?

Overview 1

Directions

1. Repeat the phrases after your teacher, making notes about intonation and stress.
2. Find some of these expressions in the model conversation on pages 4 and 5 and underline them.
3. Try to think of more expressions to add to the Overview.

Introducing yourself to the class

1. Hi, my name is (Toshiyuki). Please call me (Toshi).

2. Hello, everyone. My name is (Sami al Warah). I'd like to be called by my first name, (Sami).

3. Hi. My name is written (R-I-C-A-R-D-O), but it's pronounced "(Hicardo)."

4. It's really nice to meet everybody. I'm (Carlos).

5. I'd like to introduce myself

6. _____

Telling something about yourself

1. I'm from (Okinawa), which is in the (south) of (Japan).

2. I've been here for (six months).

3. I'm planning to (transfer to a four-year college and study journalism).

4. I'm really looking forward to (studying together this semester).

5. _____

6. _____

Practice 1.1: Play an introduction circle game

Directions

Everyone stand up and form a circle. Try to catch a ball when it is thrown to you. When you catch it, use expressions from Overview 1 on page 6 to do the following:

1. say "It's nice to meet you, (*name of person who threw the ball*)"
2. introduce yourself
3. tell something about yourself
4. throw the ball to someone else

Each time you catch the ball, introduce yourself again but tell something new about yourself.

Practice 1.2: Introduce yourself using a "me" bag *homework*

Directions

Take a brown paper shopping bag (or a different kind of bag if it has meaning for you) and decorate the outside with drawings, pictures, or words cut from magazines—whatever you think represents "you."

For example:

a photograph from home

a sketch of a cat to represent your cat

a wrapper from a chocolate bar (you love chocolate)

an exam paper (because you hate exams)

an advertisement for a car you'd like to buy

Inside the bag put photos and other things you can use to tell the class about yourself.

For example:

photographs of important people in your life

things that represent hobbies (a tennis ball)

Bring the bag to class and tell your classmates about what is outside and inside it and why you chose each item.

SECTION 2: WORKING WITH PARTNERS

Preview Questions

1. What are foreign language classes like in your country? (For example, do teachers usually lecture and students listen and take notes? Do students practice in pairs or small groups? Do students listen to tapes in a language lab? Do teachers drill the students one by one?)

2. In this class, you will often practice in pairs or small groups . . . what do you like about this?

3. What do you dislike about working in pairs or small groups?

4. Does practicing with another non-native speaker improve your English? Why or why not?

Overview 2

Directions

1. Repeat the phrases after your teacher and make notes about intonation and stress.
2. Find some of these expressions in the model conversation on pages 4 and 5 and underline them.
3. Try to think of more phrases to add to the Overview.

Offering to work together

1. Do you have a partner? Let's work together.

2. Can I join your group?

3. Can I be your partner?

4. Do you want to be "A" or "B"?

5. _____

6. _____

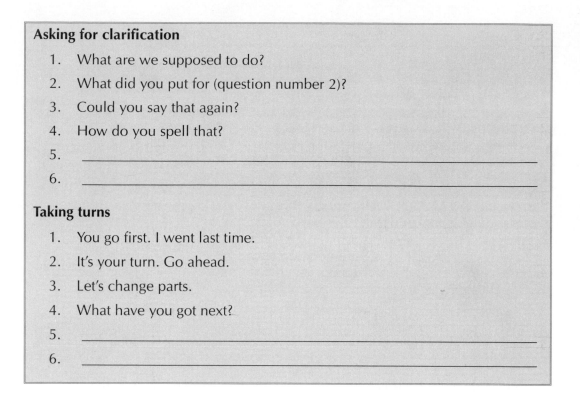

Asking for clarification

1. What are we supposed to do?
2. What did you put for (question number 2)?
3. Could you say that again?
4. How do you spell that?
5. _____
6. _____

Taking turns

1. You go first. I went last time.
2. It's your turn. Go ahead.
3. Let's change parts.
4. What have you got next?
5. _____
6. _____

Practice 2.1: Work with a partner and get to know each other better

Directions

A. Use expressions from Overview 2 on page 9 to find a partner.

B. 1. Ask your partner his (or her) name, where he's from, how long he's been here, and what he's planning to do in the States in the future (for example, plans for travel, study, or work).
   2. Take notes on the answers in the chart below.
   3. Then your partner will interview you.
   4. Use expressions from Overview 2 on page 10 to ask for clarification and take turns.

C. Change partners when your teacher tells you to. Interview as many classmates as you can.

NAME	WHERE FROM	HOW LONG HERE	FUTURE PLANS IN U.S.
1.			
2.			
3.			
4.			
5.			
6.			
7.			
8.			
9.			
10.			

Practice 2.2: Do a pair dictation, "A Stereotype about Americans"

A stereotype is an image we have about the "typical" member of some "group."
This group might be a race, a religion, a culture, a sex, or an occupation.
The pair dictation that follows is about a stereotype of American eating habits.

Directions

A. 1. One partner should look at this page. The other partner should look at page 13. Do not look at your partner's page.
   2. Read the sentence you have to your partner. Then your partner will read you the sentence you are missing. Listen to your partner and fill in the blanks. Take turns reading and writing until you have completed the paragraph.
   3. Use expressions from Overview 2 on pages 9 and 10 to take turns and clarify meaning.

Student A look here:

Use these words to tell your partner what punctuation to use:

. = period   ? = question mark
, = comma   ' = apostrophe

Example

Read sentence 1 as follows:
   "Popcorn for dinner. Question mark."

1. Popcorn for dinner? **2.** _____

_____

3. But one foreign student said that all he got for dinner one night at his

American homestay was popcorn. **4.** _____

_____

5. But then his friends said their host families ate mostly junk food everyday,

too. **6.** _____

_____

7. That certainly doesn't sound like my family. **8.** _____

_____

9. I hope foreign students realize that not all Americans eat at MacDonald's
every day.

12

Student B look here:

Use these words to tell your partner what punctuation to use:

. = period   ? = question mark

, = comma   ' = apostrophe

Example

> Read sentence 2 as follows:
> "I've never heard of such a thing. Period."

1. _____

2. I've never heard of such a thing. **3.** _____

_____

4. At first, I thought he was joking. **5.** _____

_____

6. They said that if you stay with an American family, you should expect lots of pizza, hamburgers, and TV dinners. **7.** _____

_____

8. In fact, at my house we are vegetarians and eat only natural foods.

9. _____

_____

B. Discuss these questions about the dictation:

    1.   What did the foreign students say about American eating habits?

    2.   Does the author agree with that stereotype? Why or why not?

    3.   Do you agree with that stereotype? Why or why not?

SECTION 3: DISCUSSING CULTURAL DIFFERENCES AND STEREOTYPES

Preview Questions

1. Has anyone asked you a question recently about your country? If so, what was the question? How did the question make you feel? Why?

2. Have you tried to explain about something that is different in your country, or culture, to anyone recently? If so, what did you try to explain? How did the person react?

Overview 3

Directions

1. Repeat the phrases after your teacher, making notes about intonation and stress.
2. Find some of these expressions in the model conversation on pages 4 and 5 and underline them.
3. Try to think of more expressions to add to the Overview.

Asking "delicate" questions politely

1. I hope you don't mind my asking, but (do most people sleep in hammocks) in your country?

2. I'm afraid I don't know much about (Brazil), but (do people in your country still wear traditional costumes)?

3. Is it true that (you call your friends your "mates")?

4. Aren't most of the people in your country (Buddhist)?

5. _I heard that . . ._

6. _____

Responding to stereotypes about your culture

1. I guess that used to be the custom, but nowadays (we sleep in beds).

2. There might be some people who (wear traditional costumes), but most people (wear jeans and T-shirts).

3. You must be thinking of (Australia). We don't (say that in the U.S.).

4. Well, actually, (it really depends on the person).

5. _Not anymore_

6. _____

Practice 3.1: Practice asking polite questions

Directions

Use the phrases in Overview 3 on page 14 to ask your teacher polite questions about these stereotypes of Americans.

1. Americans have guns in their homes.
2. Americans live in big houses.
3. Americans love fast-food restaurants.
4. American workers don't work hard.
5. Americans are big and tall.
6. Americans are Christians.
7. Americans watch TV for hours every day.
8. The standards are low in American public schools.
9. Americans are blond and have blue eyes.
10. American women don't like to stay home and take care of their children.

Practice 3.2: Do a role-play about how to respond to stereotypes

Directions

1. Find a partner and role-play asking about and responding to stereotypes politely. Use expressions from Overview 3, page 14.
2. One of you is Student A and the other is Student B.

   Student A: Ask Student B a question about a stereotype you have heard about his or her country.

   Student B: Try to explain to Student A why the stereotype is not true.

3. Do your role-play in front of the class.

Practice 3.3: Have a discussion about stereotypes

Directions

Discuss the following questions in a group of three or four students. Report your answers to the class.

1. Why do you think people have stereotypes about other countries?
2. Can you think of any stereotypes you had, or have heard, about the U.S.?
3. Have you heard any stereotypes about your country?
4. What is harmful about stereotypes?
5. How can we try to change stereotypes about our country or culture?

REVIEW OF OVERVIEW EXPRESSIONS

Directions

1. Write one word in each of the blanks in the following conversation.
2. After you fill in all the blanks, compare your answers with those of a classmate.
3. Together, compare your answers with those in the Overviews on pages 6, 9, 10, and 14.
4. Read the conversation together.

(Two students are introducing themselves and checking their test answers together in class.)

Carlos: Do you have a **1.** _____ ?

Toshi: No, let's work **2.** _____ .

Carlos: What's your name?

Toshi: **3.** _____ Toshiyuki, but please **4.** _____ me Toshi.

Carlos: Well, it's **5.** _____ to meet you, Toshi. I'm Carlos. Where **6.** _____ you **7.** _____ ?

Toshi: I'm from Kumamoto, which is in the south of Japan. How about you?

Carlos: I'm from Mexico.

Toshi: I hope you don't **8.** _____ my asking, but is it **9.** _____ that your country is very dry?

Carlos: Well, **10.** _____ , the north of Mexico is very dry, but the south even has rain forests.

Toshi: Oh, I see. Well, let's check these answers.

Carlos: Okay, you **11.** _____ first. What did you put for number 1?

● ●

Activity 1: Write a poem about your partner

Directions

A. Interview your partner using the following questions. Write your
    partner's answer.

    1. What's your first name?

    2. Tell me about someone you are close to in your family. What is his or
        her name?

    3. Tell me about your hometown. What is something special about it?

    4. What are some different adjectives you could use to describe yourself?
        (Give four.)

    5. Tell me about some activities, people, or ideas that you love. (Name at
        least three.)

    6. What famous person or place would you like to see someday?

    7. How are you different from the "typical" image or stereotype of people in
        your country?

    8. What's your last name?

B. Use the information you learned during the interview to make a poem
    introducing your partner to the rest of the class. Look at the structure of
    the poem and the two examples.

Figure 1: Structure of poem

MY PARTNER

Line 1: (*partner's first name*)

Line 2: DAUGHTER (*or son, sister, brother*) OF (*name*)

Line 3: RESIDENT OF (*hometown*), WHERE (*something special*)

Line 4: (*four adjectives that describe your partner*)

Line 5: LOVER OF (*give three things, people, or ideas*)

Line 6: WHO WOULD LIKE TO SEE (*famous person or place*) SOMEDAY

Line 7: WHO IS (*nationality*), BUT DOESN'T (*an example of how she or he is
         different from national stereotypes*)

Line 8: (*partner's first and last name*)

Examples of Partner Poems

Example 1:

Hae-Soo

Daughter of Jinheong

Resident of Seoul, where the 1988 Olympics were held

Ambitious, positive, responsible, cooperative

Lover of butter pecan ice cream, praise, and her black cat

Who would like to see Nelson Mandela and Paris

Who is Korean, but doesn't always eat kimchi

Hae-Soo Kim

Example 2:

Kristie

Daughter of Thomas

Resident of Mount Vernon, Washington, where the tulip fields are beautiful

Dark, wild, happy, free

Lover of dogs, oil pastels, and her boyfriend James

Who would like to see Michael Jordan and the Egyptian pyramids

Who is American, but doesn't like baseball

Kristie Parks

C. Practice your poem out loud several times. Then read it to the class.

Activity 2: Interview someone outside class about their culture and stereotypes

Directions

Interview someone in English using the following questions. If possible, interview someone from a different country who is not in your class. Take a few notes to help you remember the conversation. Feel free to change or add questions during your conversation. You will use the information from this interview in Activity 4.

1. What are your favorite holidays? Why? Could you describe how you or your family celebrate them?

2. Have you ever travelled to another country?

   Yes: Tell me about it! Where did you go? When did you go? What interesting things did you see or do? Did you see anything that surprised you? Did you miss anything from home?

   No: Where would you like to travel? Why? What would you be nervous about? What do you know about that place and the people?

3. I hope you don't mind my asking, but what's your family's ethnic background?

4. We've been talking about stereotypes in class. Could you explain to me what a stereotype is? Why do you think people have stereotypes?

5. How would you describe the "typical person" of your country? How do you feel you are different from this typical person?

6. Is there anything that you would like to ask me about my culture?

Activity 3: Keep an oral journal

Directions

On audiocassette, record a report of what you learned during your interview. Turn it in to your teacher. Remember to:

_____ talk for 3 to 5 minutes

_____ Don't tell about the whole interview. Just tell about one or two things you thought were the most interesting.

_____ Don't read a written report. Just speak. If you can't think of what to say, stop the recorder for a minute.

Activity 4: Evaluate your work.
How well do you know your classmates?

Directions

Circle your answers to the questions.

1. Do you know the names of all your classmates?

   Yes   Some   Not yet

2. Can you pronounce their names correctly?

   Yes   Some   Not yet

3. Do you remember where each classmate comes from?

   Yes   Some   Not yet

4. Do you remember a hobby or interest of each classmate?

   Yes   Some   Not yet

5. Have you learned something new about their country, culture, or region?

   Yes   Some   Not yet

6. Are you ready to talk to new people about your country or culture?

   Yes   Some   Not yet

If you couldn't answer yes to all the questions, take the time to talk to the classmates you don't know well. Ask more about their background, interests, and culture.

CHAPTER TWO

ACTIVELY LEARNING VOCABULARY

In this chapter, you will learn how to:

- ask someone to repeat words and explanations
- ask someone to explain words and meanings
- ask how to spell and pronounce new vocabulary
- check to see if you have understood

RHYTHM PRACTICE

In this chant, you will be introduced to some expressions and strategies that can help you understand and use new vocabulary.

▣ Directions

1. Listen to the chant.
2. Repeat after your teacher.
3. Practice the chant several times with a partner. One of you reads A, and the other reads B. Replace the words in parentheses with information about yourselves.

A: WHAT'S your first NAME?
WHAT'S your first NAME?

B: Could you rePEAT that, PLEASE?
Could you rePEAT that, PLEASE?

A: SURE, I said "WHAT'S your first NAME?"
"WHAT'S your first NAME?"

B: What does "FIRST NAME" mean?
What does "FIRST NAME" mean?

A: NOT your FAMily name, but your OWN name
NOT your FAMily name, but your OWN name

B: It MEANS "my OWN name"?
It MEANS "my OWN name"?

A: YEAH. Do you GET it?
YEAH. Do you GET it?

B: Oh, I get it
Oh, I get it NOW!

It's (*B's first name*)

A: HOW do you proNOUNCE it?
HOW do you proNOUNCE it?

B: (*Pronounce B's name*)
(*Pronounce B's name*)

A: HOW do you SPELL it?
HOW do you SPELL it?

B: (*Spell B's name*)
(*Spell B's name*)

A: Oh, I get it
Oh, I get it NOW!

Nice to MEET you (*B's name*).
Did I SAY that RIGHT?

B: YEAH! Nice to meet YOU, TOO.

• •

Directions

1. Read the conversation silently.
2. Listen to the conversation.
3. Read it out loud twice with a classmate, changing parts each time.
4. Answer the questions that follow.

(Toshi missed class today. He tries to call a classmate to find out what he missed in class and what assignments he has for homework.)

Toshi: *(talking to himself and dialing the telephone)* Let's see. Sami's number is 7-3-4-9-9-7-1. *(The phone rings twice, then is answered.)*

Answering Machine: You have reached 734-9971. We can't come to the phone right now, but if you'd like to leave a message and your phone number after the beep, we'll call you back as soon as possible. . . . *Beep!*

Toshi: Hi Sami, this is Toshi from your Listening and Speaking class. Sorry I missed you, but I was hoping you could tell me what I missed in class today. Call me back when you get in. My number is 733-2339. It's Tuesday, 3:30. Talk to you later.

(A couple of hours later, Sami calls back. The phone rings.)

Toshi: Hello?

Sami: Hi, Toshi? This is Sami.

Toshi: Hey, Sami. Thanks for calling back.

Sami: Yeah, I just got your message. Are you O.K.? I noticed you weren't in class.

Toshi: I'm fine; something came up. Did I miss anything in Listening and Speaking class today?

Sami: Yeah, you'd better read pages 31 and 32, we did them in class.

Toshi: I'm sorry, could you say those pages again?

Sami: Pages 31 and 32. And don't forget to rehearse your speech for tomorrow.

Toshi: I'd forgotten about the speech! Hey, what does she mean by "rehearse"?

Sami:	You know, practice giving your speech.
Toshi:	O.K., I get it. Did anything else get assigned?
Sami:	Well, we're supposed to make up interview questions on censorship.
Toshi:	Could you repeat that? CEN-what?
Sami:	CENsorship.
Toshi:	How do you spell that?
Sami:	C-E-N-S-O-R-S-H-I-P.
Toshi:	CENsorship. Did I say that right?
Sami:	Yeah.
Toshi:	What does censorship mean, anyway?
Sami:	It's too hard to explain; you'd better look it up in your dictionary!
Toshi:	O.K. Hey, thanks a lot for your help.
Sami:	No problem. See you tomorrow. You'll be there, right?
Toshi:	You bet! See you.
Sami:	Bye.

Questions on the Model Conversation:

1. How did Toshi ask Sami to repeat the page numbers he needed to read for Listening and Speaking homework?

2. What expression does Toshi use that means "I understand"?

3. Toshi asked Sami about the meaning of "rehearse" and "censorship." What phrases did he use to ask?

4. Toshi learned the spelling and pronunciation of the word "censorship." What exactly did he ask?

5. What question did Toshi use when he wanted to hear a sentence again?

* *

Preview Questions

1. Is it easier for you to understand written or spoken English? Why do you think this is so?

2. How did you study English vocabulary in your home country? Will you study vocabulary differently when you are in an English speaking country? How?

3. How can you improve your listening comprehension? Can you think of other ways?

4. What words or sounds are difficult for you to pronounce? How can you improve your pronunciation?

Overview 1

Directions

1. Repeat the phrases after your teacher, making notes about intonation and stress.
2. Find some of these expressions in the Model Conversation on pages 24 and 25 and underline them.
3. Try to think of more expressions to add to the Overview.

Asking the pronunciation of a word

1. How do you say (this word)?

2. Could you tell me the pronunciation of (this word)?

3. Could you tell me how to pronounce (this word)?

4. <u>Can you repeat that slower?</u>

Asking the spelling of a word

1. How do you spell (that word)?

2. Could you spell that for me?

3. How do you write that?

4. _____

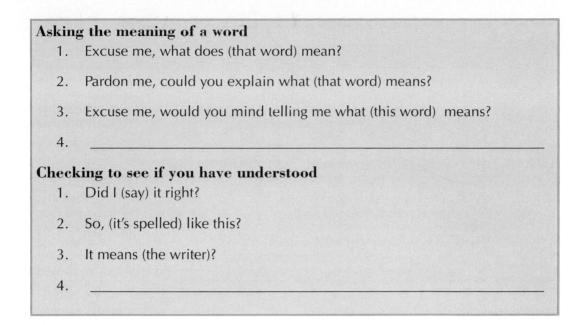

Asking the meaning of a word
1. Excuse me, what does (that word) mean?

2. Pardon me, could you explain what (that word) means?

3. Excuse me, would you mind telling me what (this word) means?

4. _____

Checking to see if you have understood
1. Did I (say) it right?

2. So, (it's spelled) like this?

3. It means (the writer)?

4. _____

Practice 1.1 : Make a vocabulary list

Directions

1. Your teacher is going to dictate a list of words to you. Take turns asking about the spelling. Use expressions from the Overview on page 26.

Example

Your teacher will say:	intonation
You should ask:	How do you spell that? (or use another expression from page x-ref.)
Your teacher will say:	I-N-T-O-N-A-T-I-O-N.

VOCABULARY LIST	
1.	6.
2.	7.
3.	8.
4.	9.
5.	10.

2. Refer to page 45 to see how well you understood the spellings.

Practice 1.2 : Check your pronunciation

Directions

1. Take turns asking your teacher to check your pronunciation of the vocabulary words on the list you just completed. Use phrases from the Overview on pages 26 and 27.
2. Repeat this practice with a partner.

Example

Student:	Could you tell me how to pronounce word number 1?
Teacher:	It's pronounced, "SYL la bus."
Student:	"SYL la bus." Did I say it right?
Teacher:	Just fine.

Practice 1.3 : Ask about the meaning of a word

Directions

1. With a partner, take turns asking and explaining about the meaning of vocabulary words. Each of you will look at a different chart.
2. Use the expressions from the Overview on pages 26 and 27.
3. Take notes on the empty lines in your chart.

Student A look here:

1. participate: ask questions and volunteer your ideas in class

2. be attentive: _____

3. skip: miss class for no good reason

4. procrastinate: _____

5. doze off: fall asleep for a few minutes

6. be tardy: _____

7. syllabus: an information sheet about a class

8. appropriate: _____

9. be supportive: help and encourage others

10. positive attitude: _____

Student B look here:

1. participate: _____

2. be attentive: listen and watch carefully

3. skip: _____

4. procrastinate: put off doing something until the last minute

5 doze off: _____

6. be tardy: be late

7. syllabus: _____

8. appropriate: good for that situation

9. be supportive: _____

10. positive attitude: believe that you can do what is needed

SECTION 2: MAKING SURE YOU UNDERSTAND

Preview Questions

1. Have you ever felt embarrassed or confused because you didn't understand what a native speaker was explaining to you? Tell what happened.

2. How do you feel about asking someone to explain when you haven't understood? Do you ever just nod your head even if you really don't understand? Why or why not?

3. Do teachers want students to ask questions? Why or why not? When is it appropriate to ask?

4. Why is it difficult to communicate in English on the telephone? What can you do when you don't understand?

Overview 2

Directions

1. Repeat the phrases after your teacher, making notes about intonation and stress.
2. Find some of these expressions in the Model Conversation on pages 24 and 25 and underline them.
3. Try to think of more expressions to add to the Overview.

Asking for repetition

1. Could you repeat that, please?

2. Would you mind repeating that, please?

3. I'm sorry, I didn't catch that.

4. _____

5. _____

Asking for explanation

1. I don't understand what you mean by (rehearse). Could you explain that?

2. I'm still not sure what you mean. Would you mind explaining that again?

3. I'm afraid I don't understand. Do you think you could explain that?

4. _____

Telling someone you understand

1. Oh, I see.

2. Oh, I get it.

3. Okay, I understand now.

4. _____

Practice 2.1: Role-play talking about class expectations

Student A look here:

Role-play #1 Directions

A. Imagine you are the teacher. Your partner is your "student." Read the class expectations to your student, and explain the meaning of the expectation when your student asks you. Your student will take notes and ask questions.

Classroom Expectations	Meaning
1. "Class participation is important in this class."	You should ask questions, volunteer your ideas, and work on class activities.
2. "You should be attentive to others."	You should pay attention when your teacher or classmates are speaking.
3. "You shouldn't skip class unless you're sick."	Come to class every day; only miss class if you're sick.
4. "Don't procrastinate about doing your homework."	You shouldn't put off doing homework that is due soon.
5. "You shouldn't doze off in class."	Don't sleep when you should be listening to the teacher or your classmates.

Student B look here:

Role-play #1 Directions

1. Take notes while partner A role-plays as the teacher.
2. Use various expressions from Overview 2 on pages 30 and 31 to ask for repetition and explanation, and to tell your "teacher" when you understand.

Classroom Expectations	Meaning
1.	
2.	
3.	
4.	
5.	

Student A look here:

Role-play #2 Directions

B. Now switch roles. In this role-play, you are a new student. Your teacher is explaining the class rules, called expectations.

1. Take notes while partner B role-plays as the teacher.
2. Use various expressions from Overview 2 on pages 30 and 31 to ask for repetition and explanation, and to tell your "teacher" when you understand.

Classroom Expectations	Meaning
1.	
2.	
3.	
4.	
5.	

Student B look here:

Role-play #2 Directions

B. Switch roles with your partner. Now, you will role-play as the "teacher." Explain to your student the following expectations for your class:

Classroom Expectations	Meaning
1. "You shouldn't be tardy."	You shouldn't be late to class.
2. "Please study the class syllabus carefully."	If you want to know about homework, exams, or grading, you should read the paper handed out on the first day of class.
3. "Visit my office at appropriate times."	You should make an appointment to see me or come during the special hours called "office hours."
4. "You should be supportive of your classmates."	You should help your classmates. You should encourage them.
5. "Please keep a positive attitude and believe in yourselves."	You should think, "Yes, I can do it!"

Practice 2.2 : Ask about homework

Directions

1. Partner A should look at the boxes named "Student A Homework 1 and 2." Partner B should look at the boxes named "Student B Homework 1 and 2."
2. Role-play the two situations and use the expressions from Overview 2 on pages 30 and 31 .

Student A look here:

Directions

A. You missed class today and are calling your friend to ask about today's homework assignments. Take notes in the "Student A: Homework 1" box. Use the expressions from pages 26, 27, 30, and 31 to ask for explanation or say that you understand.

STUDENT A: HOMEWORK 1
GRAMMAR: LISTENING AND SPEAKING: READING: WRITING:

B. Now switch roles. Your classmate was absent from class today. Answer your classmate's questions about tonight's homework. Look at the "Student A: Homework 2" box to find the information your partner needs. Prepare to explain any vocabulary your partner may not understand.

STUDENT A: HOMEWORK 2
GRAMMAR: Write ten true sentences using "modals." (Modals are verb tenses that use words like "must," or "could.")
LISTENING AND SPEAKING: Write five interview questions about "capital punishment." ("Capital punishment" means "to kill a person who did a bad crime.")
READING: No homework.
WRITING: Choose a topic from page 121 and write a descriptive paragraph. ("Descriptive" means "to tell about something and use lots of details.")

Student B look here:

Directions

A. Your classmate was absent from class today. Answer your classmate's questions about tonight's homework. Look at the "Student B: Homework 1" box to find the information your partner needs. Prepare to explain any vocabulary your partner may not understand.

STUDENT B: HOMEWORK 1
GRAMMAR: Do workbook page 47 on another piece of paper to hand in. Remember to skip lines. ("Skip lines" means "write on one line, but leave the next line empty.")
LISTENING AND SPEAKING: Write down five questions about racial discrimination. ("Racial discrimination" means "treating someone badly because of their skin color.")
READING: Continue reading your novel. The book report is due the 23rd. (You need to give your teacher a report about the novel on that date.)
WRITING: No homework.

B. Now switch roles. You missed class today and are calling your friend to ask about today's homework assignments. Take notes about your homework in the "Student B: Homework 2" box. Use expressions from pages 26, 27, 30, and 31 to ask for clarification or say that you understand.

STUDENT B: HOMEWORK 2
GRAMMAR:
LISTENING AND SPEAKING:
READING:
WRITING:

REVIEW OF OVERVIEW EXPRESSIONS

Directions

1. Write one word in each of the blanks in the following conversation.
2. After you fill in all the blanks, compare your answers with those of a classmate.
3. Together, compare your answers with those in the Overviews on pages 26, 27, 30, and 31.
4. Read the conversation together.

Teacher: Today I will choose one student to facilitate the discussion.

Wu-Mei: Excuse me, **1.** _____ you **2.** _____ that, please?

Teacher: Yes, I said that today I would choose one student to facilitate the discussion.

Wu-Mei: **3.** _____ does "facilitate" **4.** _____ ?

Teacher: It means "to lead" or "to make it go smoothly."

Wu-Mei: Oh, I see. **5.** _____ do you **6.** _____ "facilitate"?

Teacher: You spell it F-A-C-I-L-I-T-A-T-E.

Wu-Mei: **7.** _____ do you **8.** _____ it again?

Teacher: You pronounce it "facilitate."

Wu-Mei: "faCILitate." Did I **9.** _____ it **10.** _____ ?

Teacher: Yes. That was good. Any more questions? Does everyone understand? (*pause*) O.K., let's start!

Activity 1: Use a vocabulary notebook

Directions

A. Prepare a vocabulary notebook by doing the following:

1. Carry a small notebook around for a week. Whenever you hear a new word, try to ask about it and write it down.
2. In your notebook, or on a cassette tape, record the word, the meaning, and a sentence or mini-dialogue using the word.

Example

exhausted: to feel really tired
A:　　　　How are you doing?
B:　　　　I'm exhausted. I played three hours of squash today!

B. Share the vocabulary words you collected in your notebook.

1. Choose four of the most useful words you've written in your notebook this week.
2. Work with a partner and take turns explaining the vocabulary words. Use the expressions from the Overviews on pages 26, 27, 30, and 31.
3. Try to use the new words in sentences. Each partner should add these words to his or her notebook.
4. After you have finished sharing words with one partner, find a new partner. Continue until your teacher asks you to stop.

Activity 2: Role-play situations away from the classroom

Directions

With one or two partners, plan a two-minute role-play based on one of the situations below. Be sure to use expressions from the Overviews on pages 26, 27, 30, and 31. Practice with your partners and perform your role-play for the class.

Choose one of these situations:

1. Asking for directions to a friend's house on the telephone
2. Making sure you understand when your friend is showing you how to use a cash card

3. Talking to someone about renting an apartment
4. Calling a friend to ask him/her to pick up your brother at the airport tonight
5. Talking to a mechanic at a garage about what's wrong with your car
6. Talking to a nurse about your illness
7. Your own idea

Activity 3: Explain proverbs

> A proverb is an old expression, sometimes called "a saying." Proverbs often teach about life, using only a few words or phrases.

Directions

A. Play a game of "English Proverbs"

1. Study the English proverb(s) your teacher gives you. If necessary, use the expressions from the Overviews on pages 26, 27, 30, and 31 to ask about the pronunciation and meaning of your proverb.
2. In class, walk around the room telling and explaining your proverb to your classmates. Don't show the written proverb!
3. Listen and write down the other students' proverbs, the meanings, and any new vocabulary you learn.
4. At the end of the activity, check Appendix 1, page 299 to see how well you understood.

Proverb	Meaning	New Vocabulary
1.		
2.		
3.		
4.		
5.		
6.		
7.		
8.		
9.		
10.		

B. Interview an English speaker about proverbs

Use the interview on page 315 of Appendix 2 to interview an English
speaker about the meaning of the proverbs listed there.

C. Prepare to explain a proverb from your culture.

Choose a proverb that you know in your own language and prepare to teach
it to your classmates in English. Remember to:

_____ think of a proverb from your own language

_____ translate it into English

_____ prepare an explanation of its meaning

_____ prepare several examples of when you could use that proverb

_____ have someone check the grammar for you

_____ practice pronouncing and explaining vocabulary clearly

D. Practice your proverb presentation.

Before explaining your proverb to the entire class, practice explaining to a
partner in class. Notice what is difficult for your partner to understand, and
change your presentation to make it better.

Look at the following example:

Veronique: In French we say, "When the cat is gone, the mice dance."

Toshi: Could you repeat that please? "When the cat . . . ?"

Veronique: "When the cat is gone, the mice dance." It means, for example,
that when the boss is gone, the workers play.

Toshi: I'm afraid I don't understand. Could you explain?

Veronique: Well, you could use this proverb in this situation. When the
teacher leaves the room, the students stop working and start talking
and maybe they goof-off. The "cat" is the teacher and the "mice"
are the students, so "when the cat is gone the mice dance." Do you
get it?

Toshi: I think so. But, what does "goof-off" mean?

Veronique: It means to play and do funny or stupid things. Do you understand?

Toshi: I think so. When the person in charge leaves, everyone has fun?

Veronique: Yeah. That's right. What's your proverb?

E. Listening to your classmates' presentations.

1. As you listen to your classmates, write down the proverbs and notes on the meanings.
2. Use the phrases from the Overviews in this chapter to ask for repetition, explanations, and definitions.
3. Take notes on a separate piece of paper.

Example

Kathy:	"One rotten apple spoils the whole bunch."
	rotten = spoiled, not good to eat
	spoil = make bad
meaning:	One bad person can make the whole group become, or seem, bad. Example: The students had to stop bringing food to class because a couple of students left a mess.

Activity 4: Keep healthy

While you are living within a new language and culture, you may be under a lot of stress. In this activity, you will use the language you practiced in this chapter to ask questions about health resources.

Directions

A. Interview someone in English.

Use the interview form on page 316, Appendix 2 to find out about other people's strategies to fight stress, and about the resources available to help you keep healthy.

B. Learn and teach about available health resources.

1. Choose a health resource to find out about in more detail. This could be a place such as a gym, a counseling center, or a health center. Each student should choose a different place or program to visit.
2. Find all the information you can so that you can explain to your classmates and teacher. Be ready to explain:

_____ the name of the resource

_____ the location

_____ what students can expect to find there

_____ the cost

_____ the opening and closing times

_____ step-by-step how to use the resource

_____ any other important information

3. Prepare your presentation at home.
4. In front of the class, or in pairs, share what you learned about the health resource.
5. Ask questions as you listen to your classmates' presentations. Use expressions from the Overviews to make sure you understand clearly.
6. As you listen to your classmates' presentations, take notes about important information.

Example

> **Student reporting:** Wu-Mei
>
> **Name of health resource:** Biofeedback Center, MH 386
>
> **Important information:** Tel. 650–3755. Open Monday–Friday. 10–4. Free. Need appointment—call or stop by. Can use computer program to learn how to control stress or test anxiety.

Activity 5: Keep an oral journal

Directions

A. On audiocassette, explain a proverb to your teacher. Remember to:

_____ speak naturally; don't read

_____ speak for 2 to 3 minutes

_____ give examples of when you might use that proverb

_____ pronounce important vocabulary clearly

B. Describe a health resource you learned about. Remember to:

_____ speak naturally; don't read

_____ speak for 2 to 3 minutes

_____ include all the information a person would need to know in order to use that resource

Activity 6: Evaluate your work. Are you an active learner?

Directions

Evaluate your habits as a learner.

1. If I don't understand something, I ask questions:

    a) always   b) often   c) sometimes   d) never

2. If I hear a new word, I ask the meaning:

    a) always   b) often   c) sometimes   d) never

3. If I hear a new word, I ask the spelling:

    a) always   b) often   c) sometimes   d) never

4. If I learn a new word, I ask the pronunciation:

    a) always   b) often   c) sometimes   d) never

5. If I don't understand what the teacher says, I ask the teacher to repeat:

    a) always   b) often   c) sometimes   d) never

Add up your points: a= 3, b= 2, c= 1, and d= 0.

Explanation

13–15 points: BRAVO! You are a very assertive English student. You will no doubt improve your English very quickly.

9–12 points: NOT BAD. You are making an effort, but you are still a little shy. Try to speak up even more.

5–8 points: COME ON! Give yourself a push. You need to let people know when you don't understand. No one can read your mind.

0–4 points: WAKE UP. Take advantage of this opportunity you have to learn English. Ask questions—start today!

Answers

VOCABULARY LIST for Practice 1.1., page 27		
1. participation	6.	tardy
2. attentive	7.	syllabus
3. skip	8.	appropriate
4. procrastinate	9.	attitude
5. doze off	10.	supportive

CHAPTER THREE

PLANNING AND PERFORMING A ROLE-PLAY

In this chapter, you will learn how to:

- brainstorm a plot
- create roles and lines together
- rehearse a dramatic performance
- include tone of voice and non-verbal communication
- improve your performance skills

In this chant, you will practice the pronunciation of some of the vocabulary and expressions used in planning and performing a role play.

Directions

1. Listen to the chant.
2. Repeat after your teacher.
3. Practice the chant several times with a partner. One of you reads A, and the other reads B.

> **A:** WHAT do you want to DO?
> WHAT do you want to SAY?
>
> **B:** HOW do you want to DO it?
> WHO do you want to PLAY?
>
> **A:** You can be the LEADER
> I'll take NOTES.
>
> **B:** YOU can be the leader
> I'LL take notes.
>
> **A:** What happens THEN?
> What's he going to SAY?
>
> **B:** What happens NEXT?
> Want to PRACtice today?
>
> **A:** Use lots of GESTURES
> Don't be SHY.
>
> **B:** Got to SPEAK up LOUDly
> Look them in the EYE.

MODEL CONVERSATION 1

· ·

Directions

1. Read the conversation silently.
2. Listen to the conversation.
3. Read it out loud twice with two classmates, changing roles each time.
4. Answer the questions that follow.

> *(Ricardo, Veronique, and Toshi have to put on a role play about two students named Joe and Marsha and a professor named Professor Clark. They have to brainstorm a plot, think of lines, and decide roles.)*

Ricardo: So it's after class, and Joe and Marsha have just gotten their tests back. Marsha looks upset. What's going to happen?

Toshi: Joe is worried about Marsha, so he's going to ask her what's wrong.

Ricardo: What do you think, Veronique?

Veronique: Yeah, I think Joe approaches her, and why don't we say that Marsha got a really bad grade on her test, and she doesn't know what to do.

Ricardo: What kind of bad grade?

Toshi: Like a "C"?

Veronique: No, I think we should make it a "D." A "C"'s not so bad.

Ricardo: All right. So does Joe give her some advice? Like going to see her professor?

Toshi: Yes, and then Professor Clark tells her she forgot to answer two of the questions. That's why she got a "D."

Ricardo: That's good. Let's go with that. So who should speak first?

Toshi: Joe should speak first.

Ricardo: What should Joe say?

Veronique: He should say, "Marsha, what did you get on the test?"

Ricardo: Okay. And then what does Marsha say?

Toshi: She goes, "I only got a 'D.' I can't believe it!"

Veronique: That's good. I like that.

Ricardo: And what should Joe say then?

Veronique: Just a second. I haven't written down Toshi's idea yet. Okay, then Joe should say, "Why don't you talk to Professor Clark about it?"

Ricardo: That sounds good. What part do you want to play? 4

Veronique: I'll be Marsha.

Toshi: I want the one with the least lines. 6

Ricardo: You'd make a great professor, Toshi. 5

Toshi: Okay, I'll be Professor Clark, then.

Ricardo: And I'll take the part of Joe. 11

Questions on Model Conversation 1:

1. What questions does Ricardo ask to help the group brainstorm a plot?
2. How does Ricardo ask about each character's lines?
3. What expressions do the students use to suggest lines?
4. How does Ricardo ask what parts everyone wants?
5. How does Ricardo encourage Toshi to be the professor?
6. What expressions do the students use to take parts?

SECTION 1: PLANNING A ROLE-PLAY

When you do a role-play, you pretend you are in a certain situation, and you practice what you might do in that situation. For example, you might pretend to speak on the telephone in order to practice using the telephone in English. Role-plays are different from plays on the stage, because you don't have to follow a script or memorize your lines. The point of role-plays is not to perform perfectly, but to practice new language and skills and get feedback from your classmates. You may encounter role-playing exercises from time to time in your college classes; they are also called "simulations."

Preview Questions

1. Have you ever been in a play or done a role-play before? If so, when? What was the plot or situation? Did you enjoy it?
2. Why does doing a role-play help you to remember new vocabulary and expressions?
3. What do you think it means to "brainstorm" a plot? Do you have to have perfect ideas when you are brainstorming?

Overview 1

Directions

1. Repeat the phrases after your teacher, making notes about intonation and stress.
2. Find some of these expressions in the Model Conversation on pages 49 and 50 and underline them.
3. Try to think of more expressions to add to the Overview.

Brainstorming a plot

1. What's going to happen?

2. What do you think? I think . . .

3. Or maybe . . .

4. I think that's good, let's go with that.

5. _____

6. _____

Asking about a character's lines

1. Who should speak first (next, last)?
2. What should (Ricardo) say?
3. _____
4. _____

Suggesting lines

1. (Ricardo) should speak first (next, last).
2. (Toshi) should say ("What's wrong?").
3. Let's make (the teacher) say ("you've got to be kidding").
4. And then the student goes, ("No way!").
5. _____
6. _____

Asking what parts people want

1. What part do you want to take?
2. What role do you want to play?
3. Who do you want to be?
4. Which character do you want to be?
5. _____
6. _____

Taking parts

1. I'll be (the person on the skateboard).
2. I'll take the part of (the salesman).
3. I'll play the role of (Prince Charming).
4. You'd make a great (witch).
5. _____
6. _____

Practice 1: Plan a role-play

Directions

A. Make a group of three people. Look at the situation on the role-play card below. What will happen next? Brainstorm several ideas with your partners. Use expressions from Overview 1 on page 51.

ROLE-PLAY CARD

Setting: A teacher's house, at the front door.

Characters: The teacher. Two students.

Situation: The two students are going to the teacher's house for dinner. They knock at the door.

Example

A:	What's going to happen?
B:	I think the two students are bringing a huge dog to the teacher as a present, and the teacher is upset about it.
C:	Yeah, or maybe the students were not actually invited to dinner, and the teacher is in his pajamas.
A:	I think that's good, let's go with that. So what happens?

Ideas you brainstormed:

B. Now decide which character you will play in your role-play. Use expressions from Overview 1 on page 52.

Character   **Played by (classmate's name)**

1.

2.

3.

C. Based on the plot you came up with for your situation, think of lines for each character to say. Use expressions from Overview 1 on page 52. You will perform this role-play later.

Notes on each character's lines:

MODEL CONVERSATION 2

1. Read the conversation silently.
2. Listen to the conversation.
3. Read it out loud four times in groups of four, changing roles each time.
4. Answer the questions that follow.

(The students are rehearsing their role play now.)

Ricardo: Are we ready to practice now?

Toshi: Yes. Why don't we stand up and act it out with gestures?

(The students rehearse.)

Veronique: That was great, Toshi!

Ricardo: That's good, but let's go through it one more time.

Veronique: Okay. And everybody, remember to face the audience.

Toshi: Yeah, and Ricardo, try to look more worried when you go see the professor.

Ricardo: Okay.

Questions about Model Conversation 2:

1. What expressions do the students use to make suggestions?

2. What expression does Veronique use to encourage Toshi?

SECTION 2: REHEARSING AND PERFORMING

Preview Questions

Besides making up an interesting plot, what will make your role play:

- easy to hear?
- easy to understand (both the story and the language)?
- exciting and attention-getting?
- fun to watch?

Overview 2

Directions

1. Repeat the phrases after your teacher, making notes about intonation and stress.
2. Find some of these expressions in the Model Conversation on page 55 and underline them.
3. Try to think of more expressions to add to the Overview.

Rehearsing

1. Are we ready to practice now?
2. Let's go through it one more time.
3. Shall we rehearse?
4. Let's do it again.
5. _____
6. _____

Encouraging your group members

1. I think we've almost got it.
2. That was great!
3. Sounds good!
4. You were so (funny)!
5. _____
6. _____

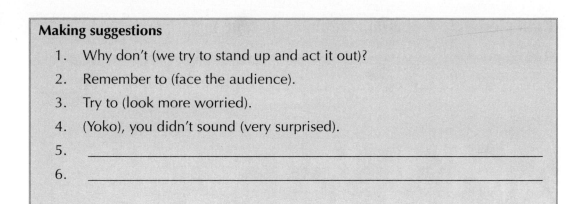

Making suggestions

1. Why don't (we try to stand up and act it out)?

2. Remember to (face the audience).

3. Try to (look more worried).

4. (Yoko), you didn't sound (very surprised).

5. _____

6. _____

Practice 2.1: Communicate through tone of voice

Directions

A. Listen to your teacher say "Well, hello" in each of the following tones of voice.

1. scared

2. happy

3. angry

4. shocked

5. tired

6. sad

B. Now, practice with a partner. Try to say the phrase, "You look very familiar" using one of the voices on the list. See if your partner can guess which one you were trying to do.

C. Your teacher will hand out a piece of paper with directions to speak in one of the voices on the list. When your teacher calls on you, say one of the lines below using the tone of voice listed on your piece of paper. Repeat your line until the class guesses which voice it is.

"Somebody, help me!"

"You look very familiar."

"That's an interesting outfit you have on."

"Could you spare a dime?"

"I never want to see you again."

Practice 2.2: Communicate through your facial expression

Directions

A. Watch your teacher demonstrate each of the following facial expressions.

1. scared
2. happy
3. angry
4. shocked
5. tired
6. sad

B. Your teacher will hand you a piece of paper with directions to make one of the facial expressions on the list.

1. Sit in a circle.
2. Each person in the circle will state some imaginary good news. When the person before you tells his or her news, respond by making the facial expression written on your paper.
3. The class should guess which facial expression you are trying to make.
4. Keep going until everyone in the circle has had a turn saying good news and responding to good news with a facial expression.

Examples of good news

"I'm getting an A!"

"I'm getting a raise!"

"I just lost five pounds!"

"I'm having a baby!"

"I just won the lottery!"

Practice 2.3: Communicate through gestures

Directions

1. You will have a message taped on your back that your classmates can read but you cannot. *
2. Walk around and let your classmates read your message. They will try to tell you the messages using only gestures (no speaking!).
3. If you guess (more or less) what the message is, your classmate can tell you and take the paper off.

Practice 2.4: Rehearse a role-play in small groups

Directions

1. Turn to your notes on page 54 about two students visiting a teacher's house for dinner.
2. With the same group members, rehearse the role-play, using expressions from Overview 2 on pages 56 and 57. Remember to:

    _____ use an expressive voice, facial expressions, and gestures for your character

    _____ encourage your group members and make suggestions

3. Perform your role-play for the class.

*Teacher: See Appendix 1, page 300 for a copy of the teacher's handout.

REVIEW OF OVERVIEW EXPRESSIONS

Directions

1. Write one word in each of the blanks in the following conversation.
2. After you fill in all the blanks, compare your answers with those of a classmate.
3. Together, compare your answers with those in the Overviews on pages 51, 52, 56, and 57.
4. Read through the conversation in a group of four.

(Carlos, Wu-Mei, Sami, and Roberta are planning and rehearsing a role-play about how to ride the city bus.)

Carlos: Okay, everybody, what do you think is going to happen?

Wu-Mei: I **1.** _____ that the foreign student is going to ask for help from the driver and passenger.

Roberta: Okay, so what do the passenger and driver do?

Sami: Let's **2.** _____ the passenger be a kind old lady who likes foreign students. She offers to tell the foreign student where to get off.

Roberta: Sounds okay. Who should **3.** _____ first?

Wu-Mei: The foreign student should **4.** _____ first.

Carlos: What does the student **5.** _____ ?

Sami: The foreign student **6.** _____ , "I'm lost. How do I get downtown?"

Carlos: That sounds good. Then what does the bus driver **7.** _____ ?

Wu-Mei: **8.** _____ make the bus driver say, "Just get on this bus. I'm going downtown."

Carlos: Okay. And then **9.** _____ does the passenger say?

Sami: Why don't we have the passenger say, "Here dear. Sit down next to me. I'll tell you when to get off the bus."

Carlos: That's good—let's **10.** _____ with that! Now, what parts do you want to take, you guys?

Wu-Mei: I'll **11.** _____ bus driver.

Sami: I'll take the **12.** _____ of the foreign student.

Carlos: Okay, I'll **13.** _____ the passenger, then. Okay, are we ready

to **14.** _____ ?

Wu-Mei: Yep. Let's try it.

(they rehearse)

Carlos: How was it?

Wu-Mei: Great, but **15.** _____ to face the driver when you speak
to him, Carlos.

Carlos: Oh, yeah. You're right. Let's go **16.** _____ it one
more time.

Activity 1: Perform a short role-play

Directions

A. 1. Make a group of three or four people.
   2. Brainstorm a 5- to 10-minute role-play about one of the following situations:

   a. a day in the life of a student in your school when everything goes wrong.

   b. a typical day in your class—Try to imitate the behavior of the students and teacher.

   c. a host family and a foreign student trying to communicate—Imagine the foreign student has just arrived and doesn't speak much English.

   d. your first day in the U.S.

   e. some of the difficulties an American might have visiting your country

   f. a talk show in which you are celebrities being interviewed

   g. a meeting between you and your group members twenty or thirty years from now

   h. "the perfect date" and "the worst date"

   i. the imaginary rags-to-riches story of one of your members (his or her rise to fame as a rock star, etc.)

   j. a conflict between parents and teenagers

B. 1. Choose roles.
    2. Rehearse, remembering to do the following:

        _____ speak loudly (try to speak so that people in the back corners can
              hear you)

        _____ face the audience (don't turn your back to the class)

        _____ think about the space you'll perform in, and if you need to rearrange
              tables or chairs

    3. Perform your role-play for the class.

C. Using the form on page 317 of Appendix 2, evaluate your classmates'
    role-plays. Give the completed evaluation form to the performers.

Activity 2: Put on a creative performance

> Try one of the following ideas for longer performances. If possible, put on your
> plays somewhere in the community.

Directions

A. Retell a folktale from your country

    1. Make a group of four to six people. Each one of you should tell a
        different folktale from your country in English.

    2. Decide which folktale would be best to perform. Consider the
        number of characters and the age of your audience.

    3. Write a script for the folktale.

    4. Perform the role play in full costume for your classmates.

    5. Perform for an audience of children.

B. Retell the end of a movie

1. Watch a movie or TV show with your class.

2. Watch the final scene twice.

3. List the characters, setting, and situation of the final scene on the board.

4. Get into groups of the number of characters in the scene and improvise or write out a different ending to the story.

5. Assign parts.

6. Rehearse and perform your new ending using gestures, expressions, voices, costumes, and props appropriate to the characters.

C. Retell your favorite comic strip

1. Write and act out a skit in English based on a comic strip or cartoons that are popular in your language. If not all your group members know the comic or cartoon, bring examples to show and explain to them.

2. Create lines, gestures, and props that show the humor of the characters.

Activity 3: Do an out-of-class interview about dramatic performance

Directions

Interview one or two people. If possible, interview someone who is not in your class and who is from a different country than you are. Be sure to tell them about your experiences, too.

You can start the interview like this:

"We are practicing role plays in our English class. Would you mind if I interviewed you for my homework? It will only take a few minutes."

1. Have you ever seen a play? If so, please tell me about your favorite play.

    a. What was the plot?

    b. What was the setting?

c. What kind of costumes did the characters wear?

d. What was a memorable scene?

2. Have you ever been in a play or done a skit or role play in front of an audience or a class?

a. If so, when was it?

b. What part did you play?

c. What was the plot?

3. Do you ever practice or rehearse before an interview, speech, or other performance?

a. If so, what techniques do you use?

Activity 4: Keep an oral journal

Directions

Record some of the most interesting points of the interview you did in Activity 3 on an audiocassette for your teacher. Remember to include:

_____ the name of the person you interviewed

_____ the most interesting answers the person gave

_____ something that surprised you

_____ something you learned from the interview

Activity 5: Evaluate your work

Directions

Circle your answers on this questionnaire.

When planning and performing my final role-play,

		Not at All				All the Time
1.	I spoke English.	1	2	3	4	5
2.	I listened carefully to my group members.	1	2	3	4	5
3.	I asked questions to help my group brainstorm a plot.	1	2	3	4	5
4.	I gave lots of suggestions to the group.	1	2	3	4	5
5.	I asked the instructor for help whenever needed.	1	2	3	4	5
6.	I practiced the role-play seriously and with energy.	1	2	3	4	5
7.	I created a voice, face, and gestures for my character.	1	2	3	4	5
8.	I faced the audience when I performed.	1	2	3	4	5

If you circled "1" or "2" for any questions, take some time to review the expressions in this chapter. Talk to your teacher and ask for more opportunities to practice the skills you are not sure of.

CHAPTER FOUR

NEGOTIATING WITH INSTRUCTORS

In this chapter, you will learn how to:

- ask about course requirements and instructor policies
- make appointments with instructors
- excuse yourself for tardiness, absences, or late or missed work
- ask about your grade in a class
- request special arrangements

RHYTHM PRACTICE

In this chant, you will practice the pronunciation of some of the vocabulary and expressions you can use to talk with your teacher about your grade.

Directions

1. Listen to the chant.
2. Repeat after your teacher.
3. Practice the chant several times with a partner. One of you reads A and the other reads B.

   A: ExCUSE me a MINute, Ms. SMITH.

   B: Yes?

   A: ExCUSE me a MINute, Ms. SMITH.

   B: Yes?

   A: Can I TALK a MOment with YOU?

   B: Yes.

   A: Can I TALK a MOment with YOU?

   B: Yes.

   A: I'm WORried about my GRADE.

   B: Yes?

A: I'm WORried about my GRADE.

B: Yes?

A: Am I DOing O.K.in the CLASS?

B: Yes!

A: Am I DOing O.K.in the CLASS?

B: Yes!

A: But I GOT an "F" on the TEST!

B: Yes.

A: But I GOT an "F" on the TEST!

B: Yes.

A: You MEAN I can STILL get an A?

B: Yes!

A: You MEAN I can STILL get an A?

B: Yes!

A: THANK you!

MODEL CONVERSATION 1

Directions

1. Read the conversation silently.
2. Listen to the conversation.
3. Read it out loud three times with two classmates, changing roles each time.
4. Answer the questions that follow.

(It is the first day in a college composition class. Ms. Ward has just finished handing out the class syllabus and describing her course.)

Ms. Ward: Are there any questions about the class? 1

Sami: *(Raises hand)* 2

Ms. Ward: Yes?

Sami: How much is the final exam worth?

Ms. Ward: About 30 percent of your grade, the same as the midterm.

Sami: What kind of exams will the final and midterm be?

Ms. Ward: Both the midterm and final will be in-class essay exams.

Wu-Mei: Excuse me, when is the paper due? 3

Ms. Ward: Papers are due the last day before finals week.

Wu-Mei: Does the paper have to be typed?

Ms. Ward: Yes.

Sami: Excuse me, I have one more question. What's your policy on attendance? 4

Ms. Ward: Participation in class discussions is an important part of the class. So attendance is very important. Attendance and participation together count for 20 percent of your grade.

Wu-Mei: *(Raises hand)*

Ms. Ward: Yes?

Wu-Mei: Do you offer extra credit?

Ms. Ward: I'm afraid I don't. *(Long pause)* Any other questions?

Questions on Model Conversation 1:

1. How does Ms. Ward invite the students to ask questions?
2. How do the students let the teacher know they have a question?
3. How does Wu-Mei ask about when to turn in her paper?
4. Sami wants to know if he has to attend class to get a good grade. How does he ask this?

SECTION 1: ASKING ABOUT COURSE REQUIREMENTS AND INSTRUCTOR POLICIES

Preview Activity

Directions

Compare typical college course requirements and instructor policies in your country with those in the U.S. Fill in the chart below. Discuss your answers in small groups.

COURSE REQUIREMENTS	MY COUNTRY	THE U.S.
1. Type of homework		Textbook readings, essays or research papers, oral presentations
2. Hours of study outside class		Two hours for every hour of class
3. Types of tests		Multiple choice and short answer questions are common in large classes; essays or oral presentations are common in small classes
4. Frequency of tests		Usually there is a final exam on the last day of class or during a special test period at the end of the term; some instructors also give a midterm exam and quizzes

5. Participation and attendance		Instructors may count your attendance and participation when deciding your grade, especially if discussion or group projects are part of the class
6. Tardiness		Some instructors may count tardiness as part of attendance, for example, "3 times late = 1 absence"
7. Acceptance of late work		Instructors may agree to accept work late or even give you an "extension" to finish it after the school term is over. You should always ask in advance, though, and have a very good reason.
8. Extra credit		Some instructors are willing to give extra points for answering certain difficult questions on a test, or for extra work a student does. Especially if you fail a test or assignment, if you have a good reason, your instructor might give you a chance to do it again, or do another, extra assignment.

Overview 1

Directions

1. Repeat the phrases after your teacher, making notes about intonation and stress.
2. Find some of these expressions in Model Conversation 1 on page 70 and underline them.
3. Try to think of more expressions to add to the Overview.

Asking for information about assignments

1. How long is the (paper) supposed to be?
2. Is the (midterm exam) going to be (multiple choice)?
3. When is the (final project) due?
4. What kind of (homework) will there be?
5. Does the (paper) have to be (typed)?
6. How many (quizzes) will there be?
7. _____
8. _____

Asking about grading

1. How much is the (final exam) worth?
2. How important is (participation)?
3. Do you count (attendance) as part of the grade?
4. What's the cut-off for (an A)?
5. _____
6. _____

Asking about policies

1. What's your policy on (attendance)?
2. Do you take points off (late assignments)?
3. Do you allow students to (retake or make up tests)?
4. Do you offer (extra credit)?
5. _____
6. _____

Practice 1.1: Ask questions about your class

Directions

Ask your teacher questions about your class to fill in the outline below. Use expressions from Overview 1 on page 74.

ASSIGNMENTS?

1. kind:

2. number:

3. length:

4. worth _____ percent of total grade

EXAMS AND/OR QUIZZES?

1. kind:

2. number:

3. worth _____ percent of total grade

OTHER GRADED WORK?

1. type:

2. number:

3. worth _____ percent of total grade

POLICY ON:

1. attendance and tardiness:

2. late assignments:

3. making up missed exams or retaking failed exams:

4. extra credit:

Practice 1.2: Role-play a professor and student

In this activity, you will take turns with a partner role-playing a student and a professor. One of you should look at Student A's part. The other should look at Student B's.

A. Role-play #1

Student A look here:

Directions

1. Pretend to be Dr. Johnson. Your partner will pretend to be your student.
2. Your partner will ask you questions about your class.
3. Answer your partner's questions about your class using the information in this syllabus.

SYLLABUS	Psychology 101	Dr. Johnson

1. **Written assignments**

    Type: Short answers to chapter questions   Due: *May 15th*

2. **Tests**

    Quizzes: *True/False*

    Final exam: *Short answer and essay questions*

3. **Grading**

    5 quizzes, worth *5* points each = 25% of total grade

    10 written assignments , *5* points each = 50%

    Final exam = *20* %

    Attendance and participation = *5* %

4. **Policy on :**

    late assignments: *not accepted*

    make-up quizzes: *not given*

    extra credit: *up to 5 points given for 3-page paper*

Student B look here:

Directions

1. Pretend to be a student in Dr. Johnson's class. Your partner will pretend to be Dr. Johnson.
2. Look at the missing information in the syllabus below. Ask your partner questions to get that information.
3. Fill in the blanks in your syllabus.

SYLLABUS	Psychology 101	Dr. Johnson

1. Written assignments

Type: Short answers to chapter questions   Due: _____ (*date*)

2. Tests

Quizzes: _____ (*what kind*)

Final exam: _____ (*what kind*)

3. Grading

_____ (*how many*) quizzes, worth _____ points each = 25% of total grade

_____ (*how many*) written assignments , _____ points each = 50%

Final exam = _____ %

Attendance and participation = _____ %

4. Policy on :

late assignments: _____

make-up quizzes: _____

extra credit: _____

B. Role-play #2

Student A look here:

Directions

1. Pretend to be a student in Ms. Lovejoy's class. Your partner will pretend to be Ms. Lovejoy.
2. Look at the missing information in the syllabus below. Ask your partner questions to get that information.
3. Fill in the blanks in your syllabus.

CLASS REQUIREMENTS AND GRADING	Intro. to Biology	Ms. Lovejoy

1. **Written assignments**

   Type: Write-ups of biology experiments   Due: _____ (*date*)

2. **Tests**

   Quizzes: _____ (*what kind*)

   Final exam: _____ (*what kind*)

3. **Grading**

   _____ (*how many*) written assignments , _____ points each = 75%

   Final exam = _____ %

4. **Policy on :**

   late assignments: _____

   _____

   attendance: _____

   _____

   extra credit: _____

   _____

Student B look here:

Directions

1. Pretend to be Ms. Lovejoy. Your partner will pretend to be your student.
2. Your partner will ask you questions about your class.
3. Answer your partner's questions about your class using the information in this syllabus.

CLASS REQUIREMENTS AND GRADING	Intro. to Biology	Ms. Lovejoy

1. **Written assignments**

   Type: Write-ups of biology experiments   Due: *by the last day of class*

2. **Tests**

   Quizzes: *none*

   Final exam: *multiple choice*

3. **Grading**

   5 written assignments , *15* points each = 75%

   Final exam = *75* %

4. **Policy on :**

   late assignments: *no assignment accepted after the final exam*

   attendance: *not counted, but experiments must be finished before the final*

   extra credit: *up to 10 points can be earned for extra experiments—*
   if interested,ask teacher

MODEL CONVERSATION 2

Directions

1. Read the conversation silently.
2. Listen to the conversation.
3. Read it out loud twice with a partner, changing roles each time.
4. Answer the questions that follow.

(Lee makes an appointment to stop by Ms. Ward's office during her office hours. He is worried because he missed the midterm exam.)

Lee:	Excuse me, Ms. Ward, may I talk to you in your office?
Ms. Ward:	Certainly. Why don't you come see me during my office hours?
Lee:	When are they?
Ms. Ward:	2 to 4, Tuesdays and Thursdays.
Lee:	Thank you. I'll try to stop by Tuesday at 3.
Ms. Ward:	Great. See you later, Lee.
Lee:	Good-bye.

(On Tuesday)

Lee:	*(Knocks on office door).* Excuse me, Ms. Ward, may I talk to you now?
Ms. Ward:	Sure, come in and sit down.
Lee:	I'm sorry I missed class last Friday. I got in a car accident on the way to school, and I had to wait for the police to arrive.
Ms. Ward:	That's terrible. Were you hurt?
Lee:	No, but my car was totaled.
Ms. Ward:	I'm sorry to hear that. It's too bad, because the midterm exam was on Friday. And the midterm counts for 30 percent of your grade.
Lee:	Really? How am I doing in the class so far?
Ms. Ward:	So far you're getting a "C."
Lee:	Is there any way I could make up the midterm?

Ms. Ward: Well . . . normally I don't give make-ups, but in this case, I can let you take the exam before class on Thursday. The topic of the essay question will be different, though.

Lee: Thank you so much!

Ms. Ward: You're welcome. Come to my office by 8 A.M. Thursday, okay?

Lee: Okay.

Questions about Model Conversation 2:

1. How does Lee ask permission to visit Ms. Ward's office?
2. What expression does Lee use to apologize for missing class?
3. What excuse does he have for missing class?
4. How does Lee ask Ms. Ward to let him make up the midterm?

SECTION 2: NEGOTIATING WITH INSTRUCTORS

Preview Activity

Directions

Fill in the table below. Discuss your answers with your classmates.

SITUATION	WHAT I DID IN MY COUNTRY IN THE PAST	WHAT I THINK I SHOULD DO IN THE U.S.
1. You get a bad grade on an assignment because you misunderstood the directions		
2. You are 30 minutes late for class		
3. You get very sick before a big test		
4. You can't finish a research paper before the due date		
5. You get a "C" in a class, but you feel you deserved at least a "B"		

Overview 2

Directions

1. Repeat the phrases after your teacher, making notes about intonation and stress.
2. Find some of these expressions in Model Conversation 2 on pages 80 and 81 and underline them.
3. Try to think of more expressions to add to the Overview.

Asking permission to speak to a teacher privately

1. May I talk to you in your office?

2. I'd like to make an appointment to talk to you.

3. Can I talk a moment with you?

4. Can I come see you in your office?

5. _____

6. _____

Arranging a time to meet

1. Let me look at my schedule.

2. How about (Wednesday at 3)?

3. I'm sorry. I'm afraid I have (a field trip all day).

4. That's good for me.

5. Why don't you come see me during my office hours?

6. _____

Apologizing and explaining

1. I'm sorry I was late for (class) today. (I got an important phone call from home.)

2. I'm sorry I missed (class) yesterday. (I wasn't feeling well.)

3. I'm sorry I missed (the test) yesterday. (I was in a car accident.)

4. I'm sorry I didn't finish (the assignment) today. (I had a test in another class.)

5. _____

6. _____

Practice 2.1: Make appointments to talk to professors

Your teacher will tell you whether you will play the role of a student or a professor. Students look at this page. Professors turn to page 86 now.

"Students" look here:

You need to make appointments to speak to five different professors.

Directions

1. Use expressions from Overview 2 on pages 83 and 84 to ask permission to speak to an instructor privately and decide on a good time to meet.
2. Look carefully at your schedule for next week; don't show your schedule to the professor.
3. Write down appointments with professors in your schedule as you make them.

STUDENT'S SCHEDULE FOR NEXT WEEK

MONDAY

classes 10 to 1

softball practice 3 to 5

TUESDAY

classes 9 to 12

lunch with Jamie

WEDNESDAY

all-day field trip

THURSDAY

classes 9 to 12

computer lab 1 to 3

softball practice 3 to 5

dinner party 6 to ?

FRIDAY

classes 10 to 1

softball game 3 to 5

party at Jeff's 7 to ?

"Professors" look here

Five different students want to make an appointment to speak to you privately.

Directions

1. Agree to meet with the student.
2. Use expressions from Overview 2 on pages 83 and 84 to decide on a good time to meet.
3. Look carefully at your schedule for next week; don't show your schedule to the student.
4. Write down appointments with students in your schedule as you make them.

PROFESSORS' SCHEDULE FOR NEXT WEEK

MONDAY

> lunch with Kate 12:30
>
> independent study meeting 2 to 3

TUESDAY

> all-day guest lecture at Jackson Community College

WEDNESDAY

> class presentations 10 to 12

THURSDAY

> meet Sophie for dinner and movie at 5:15

FRIDAY

> seminar class 10 to 1
>
> dentist appointment 3:30

Practice 2.2: Apologize and explain

Directions

Take turns apologizing for and explaining tardiness and absences. Follow the example.

Example

A:	I'm sorry I was late for class today.
	(My car wouldn't start in the morning.)
B:	I'm sorry to hear that. Thank you for telling me.

	LATE	ABSENT	REASON
1.	X		I had a dentist's appointment.
2.		X	I had to go to the doctor.
3.		X	I had the flu.
4.	X		I was caught in traffic.
5.		X	Something came up.
6.	X		I had a job interview.
7.	X		I wasn't feeling well.
8.		X	My flight was delayed.
9,	X		I had a personal emergency.
10.		X	I just couldn't make it.

Practice 2.3: Role-play a student negotiating with an instructor

Directions

Role-play one of the following situations. In your role-play, include a solution for each problem. Use expressions from Overview 2 on pages 83 and 84 to ask for special arrangements and ask about your progress in a class.

A. A student named Teresa is worried about her grade in Dr. Johnson's class because she has missed two assignments and one quiz. She asks Dr. Johnson:

- how she is doing in the class so far.

- if she can turn in her two assignments late.

- if she can make up the quiz she missed.

- if she can do any extra credit to raise her grade.

B. A student named Wu-Mei is worried about her grade in Ms. Lovejoy's class. She has missed two weeks of class, has not turned in any homework, and got an "F" on the last quiz. She tells Ms. Lovejoy she is sorry about missing class and asks:

- if being absent has affected her grade.

- if she can turn her homework in later.

- if she can make up the quiz that she got an "F" on.

REVIEW OF OVERVIEW EXPRESSIONS

Directions

1. Write one word in each of the blanks in the following conversations.
2. After you fill in all the blanks, compare your answers with those of a partner.
3. Together, compare your answers with those in the Overviews on pages 74, 83, and 84.
4. Read through the conversations together once.

A. *(Ricardo makes an appointment to see Mr. Nicholas. He has questions about an assignment and the final exam, and he is worried about his grade.)*

Ricardo: May I **1.** _____talk_____ with you in your office?

Mr. Nicholas: Certainly. **2.** _____How_____ about today at four?

Ricardo: Thank you. Good-bye.

(later)

Ricardo: Excuse me, Mr. Nicholas, may I come in?

Mr. Nicholas: Yes, Ricardo. Please sit down. What can I do for you?

Ricardo: I have some questions about the essay. When is it **3.** _____ ?

Mr. Nicholas: On May 15.

Ricardo: And how **4.** _____ is the final exam **5.** _____ ?

Mr. Nicholas: 25 percent of your grade.

Ricardo: Oh, I see. Thank you. Am I **6.** _____ O.K. in the class so far?

Mr. Nicholas: Well, your quiz scores are all "Cs," but your homework has been all "As," so you are getting a "B" so far in the class.

Ricardo: Oh, I see. And is there **7.** _____ I could do to **8.** _____ my grade?

Mr. Nicholas: Well, you might find someone to study with before the quizzes. That might help you do better on them.

Ricardo: Oh, I see. Thank you very much.

Mr. Nicholas: You're welcome. See you in class.

B. *(Hae-Soo apologizes to Ms. Ward for missing class and asks to make up a quiz.)*

Hae-Soo: Excuse me, Ms. Ward. I'm **9.** _sorry_ for missing class yesterday. I had a terrible toothache and I had to go to the dentist.

Ms. Ward: I'm sorry to hear that, Hae-Soo. I hope you're feeling better. Do you know you missed a quiz yesterday?

Hae-Soo: Yes, I know. Is there **10.** _a_ way I could **11.** _make_ up the quiz this week?

Ms. Ward: I'm sorry, but I never give make-ups. There are just too many students in the class.

Hae-Soo: Oh, I see. Thank you anyway.

● ●

Activity 1: Discuss and find solutions for problems with instructors

Directions

1. In a small group, discuss the following problems and brainstorm solutions.
2. When you are finished, share your answers with the class.
3. Discuss and/or vote on the best solutions.

Problem 1: "English Only!"

Students in Mr. Beck's English class are always speaking their native languages during small-group discussions. They only speak English when they are talking to Mr. Beck, or when they are giving speeches in front of the class. Mr. Beck has told them "English only!" over and over, but they continue to speak their first language. He sometimes loses his temper in class and the students are beginning to feel uncomfortable. Mr. Beck can't understand why they refuse to speak English to each other. What can Mr. Beck do to solve this problem?

SOLUTIONS: 1.

2.

3.

4.

Problem 2: "A Shy Student"

Sami is afraid he will get a low grade in his Anthropology class because he doesn't speak much in group discussions. At the beginning of the term, the instructor said that participation in group discussions counted for 20 percent of the final grade. He wants to speak, but he can't always follow the conversation of the American students, and also he is shy about speaking in English. What can he do?

SOLUTIONS: 1.

2.

3.

4.

Problem 3: "The biggest problem students have in dealing with instructors"

In your small group, try to think of another problem that some of you have had getting along with an instructor. Write it down here. Then think of some solutions.

PROBLEM:

SOLUTIONS: 1.

2.

3.

4.

Activity 2: Discuss cheating and plagiarizing

"Cheating" means copying someone else's answers, or letting someone copy your answers, on a test or assignment. It also means bringing in answers to a test without the instructor's permission.

"Plagiarizing" means copying an author's words and not saying who wrote them, but pretending they are your own words. Both cheating and plagiarizing are considered to be very serious, like crimes, in American schools. Students can even be kicked out (expelled) from school for these forms of "academic dishonesty."

Directions

Fill in the chart below about your own country and the U.S. Discuss your answers in small groups. Be sure to say why you think the actions described are O.K. or not.

SITUATION	IN MY COUNTRY	IN THE U.S.
1. Is it O.K. if you help your classmate with his or her homework?		
2. Is it O.K. if you let your classmate copy your homework answers?		

3. Is it O.K. if you write answers to a test on your hand?		
4. Is it O.K. if you ask a classmate about the directions on a quiz during the quiz?		
5. Is it O.K. if you turn in a research paper you wrote for a class last year for a grade in a class this year?		
6. Is it O.K. if you use sentences from a book in the library in your paper?		
7. Is it O.K. if you ask a native English speaker to correct an out-of-class essay for you?		
8. Is it O.K. if you get a copy of last year's final exam and study it before the final, and it turns out to be the exact same test?		
9. Is it O.K. if you sit next to a friend during a quiz and look at his paper to see if you got the same answers?		
10. Is it O.K. if you write key concepts into a dictionary that you will use during a test?		

Activity 3: Talk to your instructor privately

Directions

Make an appointment with your instructor to discuss:

1. how your grade or achievement in the class is decided
2. your achievement so far
3. any absences or missed work
4. how you could improve your performance
5. anything about the class you do not understand

Before your appointment, fill out the self-evaluation on page 318, Appendix 2, and bring it to your appointment to show your teacher.

Activity 4: Get advice about communicating with instructors

Directions

A. Use the questions below to interview someone who is already taking college classes. Try to find someone who might be able to give you some good advice about communicating with instructors.

You can start the interview like this:

"We are discussing how to do well in college in my English class. Would you mind if I interviewed you for my homework? It will only take a few minutes."

1. Could you show me any syllabi from classes you are taking? What kind of assignments and exams do you have? How does the instructor decide your grade?
2. Have you ever been late to or absent from a class before? What were the reasons? Did you talk to the instructor about it? Why or why not?
3. What is the best way to catch up with a class if you have been absent, especially if you have missed homework or quizzes?
4. What should you do if you know you are not going to be able to finish a project by the deadline?
5. What would you do if you got a lower grade on something than you expected?
6. (*Your own question*)

B. Give a brief report about your interview with a college student. Remember to include the following in your report:

_____ 1. some information about the person you interviewed

_____ 2. what advice he or she gave you

_____ 3. what you thought about his or her advice

_____ 4. what you now know about dealing with instructors

_____ 5. what you still need to know about dealing with instructors

Activity 5: Give a short presentation about a favorite teacher

All teachers are different, and everyone probably has a different idea about what a good teacher is. Most of our ideas are based on our past experiences as students.

Directions

Draw a picture of one of your favorite teachers from the past below. You can draw just a face, or a whole body. You can also cut out pictures from magazines or other places to use in your portrait. Show the class your picture, and tell them:

_____ 1. why you liked this teacher

_____ 2. a special memory you have of this teacher

_____ 3. what a good teacher is, in your opinion

Activity 6: Interview someone about their favorite teacher

Directions

Ask someone to draw a picture of a teacher he or she liked and tell you why he or she liked that teacher. If possible, try to interview someone who is not in your class and who is from a different country than you are.

Sample questions:

1. Why did you like this teacher?

2. Tell me about a special memory you have of this teacher.

3. In your opinion, what makes a good teacher?

4. _____

5. _____

(Think of other questions you'd like to ask.)

Activity 7: Keep an oral journal

Directions

In your oral journal, compare your favorite teacher with the favorite teacher of the person you interviewed. Remember to do the following when you record your oral journal:

_____ speak for 2 to 3 minutes

_____ speak naturally (do not read)

_____ point out something you found in common between the person you interviewed and yourself

_____ point out something different

_____ tell about something you realized from your interview

Activity 8: Evaluate your work

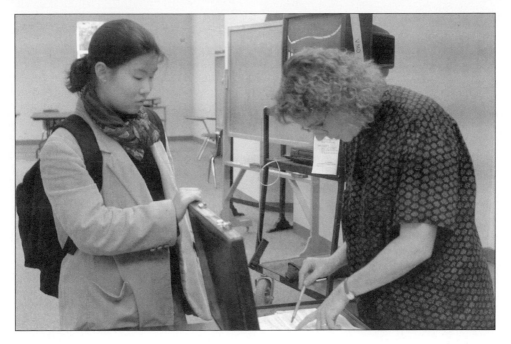

Directions

Circle your answers on this questionnaire.

Do you feel confident:

1. asking questions about course requirements and policies?

    Yes   Somewhat   Not yet

2. asking to speak to your instructor?

    Yes   Somewhat   Not yet

3. apologizing for and explaining your absences or tardiness to your instructor?

    Yes   Somewhat   Not yet

4. asking about your grade?

    Yes   Somewhat   Not yet

5. asking for special arrangements?

    Yes   Somewhat   Not yet

If you couldn't answer yes to all the questions, take some time to review the expressions in this chapter. Talk to your teacher and ask for more opportunities to practice the skills you are not sure of.

CHAPTER FIVE

GIVING A DEMONSTRATION

In this chapter, you will learn how to:

- Give a clear, interesting explanation on how to do something
- Introduce and give background information for a demonstration
- Clearly communicate what you want your audience to do, and not do
- Invite participation from your audience
- Give encouragement

RHYTHM PRACTICE

In this chant, you will be introduced to some vocabulary and structures you can use when you give a demonstration.

Directions

1. Listen to the chant.
2. Repeat after your teacher.
3. Practice the chant several times with a partner. One of you reads A, and the other reads B.

A: TEACH you, TEACH you, I want to TEACH you
TEACH you, TEACH you, I want to TEACH you.

B: SHOW you, SHOW you, I want to SHOW you
SHOW you, SHOW you, I want to SHOW you.

A: LEARN it, TRY it, GIVE it a GO, now!
LEARN it, TRY it, GIVE it a GO, now!

B: HOW to end, HOW to start, Want to have YOU take PART
HOW to end, HOW to start, Want to have YOU take PART.

A: WATCH me, WATCH me, We'll do it ALL aGAIN
WATCH me, WATCH me, We'll do it ALL aGAIN.

B: MAKE sure, MAKE sure, Make sure you've GOT it NOW
MAKE sure, MAKE sure, Make sure you've GOT it NOW.

A: YOU try it, YOU try it, You can DO it now!
YOU try it, YOU try it, You can DO it now!

B: GREAT job! GOOD try! Now you've GOT it DOWN!
GREAT job! GOOD try! Now you've GOT it DOWN!

● ●

Directions

1. Read the model silently.
2. Listen to the model.
3. Read it out loud with a classmate, taking turns reading the paragraphs.

(Ms. Ward has written vocabulary words on the board, and has brought ingredients for making popcorn to class.)

Ms. Ward: The name of my demonstration is "How to Make Healthy Popcorn." I chose this topic because popcorn is a very American food. Corn originated in the Americas, and the native Americans taught the first European settlers how to grow corn.

Traditionally, we cook popcorn in hot oil and cover it with butter and salt. I'd like to show you how to make popcorn with a hot air popcorn-maker. *(shows the class the machine)* Cooked this way, popcorn can be very low calorie and nutritious. *(points to the word "nutritious")* Nutritious means good for your body and your health.

First, preheat the popcorn-maker. *(points to the word "preheat" on the board)* Preheat means to turn on the heat early, before you want to cook. Plug in the cord *(shows where the plug is in the wall socket)* about five minutes before you start the popcorn. I plugged it in a few minutes ago, so it is almost ready.

After the machine is preheated, you can start. Can I have a volunteer to help me? *(someone volunteers)*

Next, measure the popcorn kernels, which are dried corn seeds. *(hands volunteer a jar of popcorn and a measuring cup)* This machine takes 1/3 of a cup.

After that, pour the kernels into the machine. *(volunteer helps)*

That's great. Next, push the lever. *(points to the word "lever," and to the lever on the machine; volunteer pushes it and the kernels fall into the machine)*

Make sure to put a bowl under the chute *(points to the word on the board and shows the chute on the machine)* before the popcorn starts popping, or you will get popcorn everywhere! *(volunteer places bowl under chute)*

While we are waiting, let me show you some toppings you can put on the popcorn. *(points to "topping")* The most common topping is butter and salt, but if you want to try something a little healthier, you can use soy sauce, garlic salt, chili powder, parmesan cheese, cinnamon sugar or even Brewer's yeast. *(shows each seasoning)* Popcorn is good plain, too.

After the popcorn has finished popping, you can sprinkle the seasoning on. Sprinkle means to shake it on lightly, like this. *(They put the different toppings on the popcorn in different bowls.)*

(to the volunteer) Thanks a lot for helping. Would anyone like to try the popcorn with the different toppings? *(Ms. Ward hands around the bowls.)* How does it taste?

I hope you enjoyed learning about how to make healthy popcorn. And I hope you see what a demonstration about some part of your culture can be like. Maybe when you return to your country, you can remember me and America by making popcorn. Thank you very much.

Questions on the model conversation:

1. How did Ms. Ward introduce her topic?

2. What expressions did the teacher use to point out the steps of making popcorn?

3. Notice the words that follow "First," "Next," and "Finally." Do you need to use the word "you" before the verb?

4. How did Ms. Ward have the classmates participate in her demonstration?

5. How did Ms. Ward say "Don't forget to put the bowl under the chute"? Which expression sounds more polite?

6. How did Ms. Ward end, or "close," the demonstration?

SECTION 1: CHOOSING AND INTRODUCING YOUR DEMONSTRATION

Preview Questions

Directions

In small groups, brainstorm some appropriate demonstration topics for each of the following situations:

1. You are asked to visit an elementary school class to talk about your country. Think about what things five and six-year olds would enjoy learning about or doing. What things would be difficult for them to do?

2. You are going to a high school to be part of an international fair. You want to demonstrate something that will interest teenagers.

3. You are going to do a home-stay with an American family. Think about what you could demonstrate or talk about to the entire family.

Overview 1

Directions

1. Repeat the phrases after your teacher, making notes about intonation and stress.
2. Find some of these expressions in the Model Conversation on pages 101 and 102 and underline them.
3. Try to think of more expressions to add to the Overview.

Introducing your demonstration

1. Would you like to learn how to (bow correctly) in my country?

2. I'd like to show you how to (make my favorite food).

3. Let me tell you about how we (greet each other) in my country.

4. _____

5. _____

Practice 1.1: Choose a topic for your cultural demonstration

Directions

A. In class, or as homework, prepare answers to the following questions about your culture.

1. What special foods do you have in your country?

2. Can you explain how to make or eat these special foods?

3. What do people in your country do and say when they meet?

4. Do you wear special clothing sometimes?

5. Are there some cultural mistakes visitors to your country often make? Can you explain what they should or shouldn't do?

6. Do you have a different writing system you could demonstrate?

7. Do you know any songs, dances, sports, or games (traditional, modern, or children's) which you could teach?

8. How do you say "Hello, nice to meet you," "Thank you," or "I love you" in your language? What other phrases would be useful or interesting to learn?

9. What different gestures or expressions do people in your country use? What sound indicates pain? What gesture do you use to indicate that someone is crazy?

10. What sounds do you use to represent the sounds that animals make? Are they the same sounds as Americans use for those animals?

11. What special traditions are there for weddings?

12. What special traditions are there for major holidays?

B. Interview a partner with the questions above, and compare ideas for demonstrations.

C. Pick three of these topics that you could demonstrate to your classmates. Write them here:

1. _____

2. _____

3. _____

Practice 1.2: Introduce your topic

Directions

Make a circle. Take turns standing up and introducing the demonstration topics you selected in Practice 1.1, part C. Refer to the Overview on pages 103 and 104. Try to use different expressions each time you introduce a topic and explain why you chose it.

SECTION 2: BREAKING YOUR DEMONSTRATION INTO STEPS

Preview Questions

Directions

1. You have decided to teach something about your language. What can you teach in just ten or fifteen minutes?

2. There are many parts to the activity you want to teach. How can you help the audience understand the activity clearly?

3. You need to teach many new words during your demonstration. What can you do to help people understand and remember these new words or expressions?

Overview 2

Directions

1. Repeat the phrases after your teacher, making notes about intonation and stress.
2. Find some of these expressions in the Model Conversation on pages 101 and 102 and underline them.
3. Try to think of more expressions to add to the Overview.

Explaining new vocabulary

1. I want to introduce (some vocabulary you may not know).
2. I'd like to make sure everybody understands these words:
3. ("Onigiri") is (Japanese) for (a rice ball).
4. ("Ça va?") means ("Is everything O.K.?")
5. _____
6. _____

Using step-by-step language

1. First, (fold the paper in half), this way.
2. Next, (take the gift using both hands). Watch me.
3. After that, (hold the coffeepot in your left hand), this way.
4. Finally, (wrap the seaweed around the rice), like this.
5. _____
6. _____

Practice 2.1: Organize a demonstration

Directions

With a partner, try to put the sentences below in correct order from 1 to 11. Write "1" in the blank for the first sentence, "2" for the second, and so on.

USING THE "800" DIRECTORY

___9___ "Listed" or "listing" means that the operator can find it in her book.

___6___ Next the operator will say, "800 directory, how can I help you?"

___3___ Toll-free means that you don't have to pay for the call.

___5___ First, dial 800-555-1212.

___10___ Finally, you say thanks, hang up, and try calling that number. It won't cost you anything to call.

___8___ Next, the operator will give you the 800 number, if there is one listed.

___7___ After that, you should say the name of the business you want to call.

___1___ Today, I'd like to teach you how to find and use toll-free telephone numbers.

___2___ I chose this topic because we all want to have lower telephone bills.

___4___ Make sure to dial a "1" first, or it won't work.

___11___ Thanks for being such a good audience, and I hope your phone bills will be a little lower!

Practice 2.2: Use step-by-step language

Directions

Practice the format of a demonstration and the phrases for step-by-step explanations by teaching your partner how to do something simple.

A. Choose one of the following topics.

PARTNER A	PARTNER B
use the emergency 911 telephone number	use a credit card
put on shoes and socks	cook rice
say, "Hello. How are you?" in a different language	make a paper airplane

B. Prepare your mini-demonstration. Your demonstration should take about one minute.
   1. List the steps needed to do the activity you have chosen.
   2. Add step-by-step language. Refer to the Overview on pages 106 and 107.
   3. Decide how you will introduce your demonstration and explain why you chose that topic.

C. Practice giving the demonstration you prepared in part B. Your partner will listen and mark the checklist for you.

CHECKLIST FOR YOUR PARTNER'S PRESENTATION
_____ introduced the topic
_____ explained why topic was chosen
_____ explained vocabulary
_____ used step-by-step language
_____ warned about possible problems
_____ closed the demonstration

D. Go over the checklist with your partner. Discuss how you could improve your demonstration. Listen carefully to your partner's advice, and practice one more time.

SECTION 3: ENCOURAGING PARTICIPATION

Preview Questions

1. Like a good speech, a good demonstration is presented clearly, loudly, and with eye contact. How is a demonstration different from a speech?

2. How can you make a demonstration interesting for your audience?

3. When you give a demonstration, how can you know if your audience understands your explanation?

4. How can you help your audience master the skill you are demonstrating?

5. What can you do if someone in your audience is having trouble doing what you demonstrated?

Overview 3

Directions

1. Repeat the phrases after your teacher, making notes about intonation and stress.
2. Find some of these expressions in the Model Conversation on pages 101 and 102 and underline them.
3. Try to think of more expressions to add to the Overview.

Making sure the audience understands

1. Do you understand what I mean? Let me show you again.
2. Is that pretty clear? Should I explain again?
3. Do you have any questions?
4. Shall we go through it again?
5. _____
6. _____

Inviting participation

1. Why don't you try it now?
2. Let's do it together now.
3. I think you are ready to try it!
4. Would you like to try it?
5. _____
6. _____

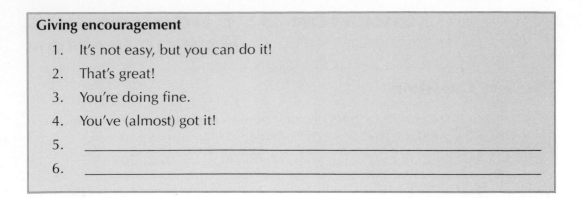

Giving encouragement

1. It's not easy, but you can do it!
2. That's great!
3. You're doing fine.
4. You've (almost) got it!
5. _____
6. _____

Practice 3.1: Notice good performance skills

Directions

A. In exercise 2.1 on page 107, you read about how to make toll-free telephone calls. Now, listen as your teacher presents a demonstration on this topic. *

B. With a partner, discuss the following questions:

1. How was the information explained differently than in the written version on page 107?

2. Was this a better, more effective explanation? Why?

3. Could you hear the teacher clearly?

4. What objects or gestures did the teacher use during the demonstration?

5. Did the teacher check to make sure everyone understood?

6. How did the teacher get the students to participate? Did this help you understand more clearly about how to find a toll free number? Why?

7. What did your teacher do if someone made a mistake or seemed nervous or embarrassed to try?

* Teacher: See Appendix 1, page 301, for a copy of the teacher's script.

C. With a partner, look at the script of your teacher's demonstration (see page 301, Appendix 1) and do the following things:

1. Underline the phrases that the teacher uses to:
   invite participation
   give encouragement
   make sure the audience understands

2. Read the demonstration out loud with your partner.

Practice 3.2: Present a one-minute demonstration to the class

Directions

A. Add some expressions for inviting participation and giving encouragement to the mini-demonstration you prepared in Practice 2.2 on page 108. Refer to the Overview on pages 109 and 110 for help.

B. With a partner, practice your mini-demonstration. Focus on presenting it clearly and on having your partner participate. Your partner will give you feedback using the checklist below:

CHECKLIST ON YOUR PARTNER'S PERFORMANCE:

_____ spoke loudly with clear pronunciation

_____ looked at classmate(s) often

_____ used gestures or real objects to help demonstrate

_____ checked for understanding

_____ invited and encouraged participation

_____ spoke for one minute

C. Go over the checklist with your partner. Discuss how you could improve your performance. If there is time, practice again.

D. Present your demonstration to the class.

REVIEW OF OVERVIEW EXPRESSIONS

Directions

1. Write one word in each of the blanks in the following demonstration.
2. After you fill in all the blanks, compare your answers with those of a classmate.
3. Together, compare your answers with those in the Overviews on pages 103, 104, 106, 107, 109, and 110.

Today, I'd like to **1.** _____ you **2.** _____ to make a vinaigrette. "Vinaigrette" **3.** _____ French **4.** _____ a vinegar and oil salad dressing. I **5.** _____ this topic because I'm homesick for my mother's vinaigrette, and it is easy to make.

6. _____ , buy some dark olive oil, wine vinegar, fresh garlic, lettuce, salt, and pepper. **7.** _____ , wash, dry, and chill the lettuce. "Chill" **8.** _____ "to keep cool in the refrigerator."

9. _____ , peel the garlic and crush it with a fork in the bottom of the salad bowl, **10.** _____ way. Do you understand what I **11.** _____ ? Would you like to **12.** _____ it, Ricardo? (*Ricardo crushes the garlic.*)

You're **13.** _____ fine! **14.** _____ , add one tablespoon of olive oil and one teaspoon of vinegar per person, like **15.** _____ . Add salt and pepper until you like the taste. Leave the vinaigrette at room temperature. **16.** _____ you chill the vinaigrette, it **17.** _____ lose its flavor. **18.** _____ , add the chilled, dry lettuce and mix just before serving. That's all. Do you **19.** _____ any questions? Thanks for **20.** _____ such a good audience, and I hope you will try to make a vinaigrette sometime.

Activity 1: Give a detailed cultural demonstration

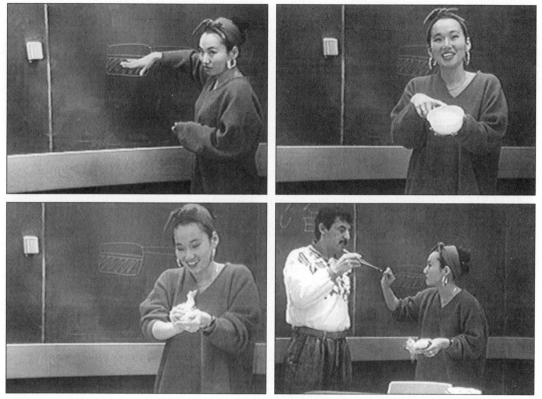

Directions

A. Choose something from your culture to demonstrate for your classmates. You may use this demonstration later with an American audience. Look at the checklist below as you prepare and practice your demonstration.

> _____ 1. The demonstration is the right length, not too short or long.
>
> _____ 2. The topic is not too big. I can explain this topic well in that much time.
>
> _____ 3. I broke the demonstration up into steps.
>
> _____ 4. I planned a way for my classmates to participate.
>
> _____ 5. I have props and can make gestures to help people understand.
>
> _____ 6. I know how to explain vocabulary my classmates might not know.
>
> _____ 7. I can pronounce all the words I will use.
>
> _____ 8. I've thought about what problems or misunderstandings might come up, and I'm ready to warn my classmates.

B. 1. Prepare everything you need for your demonstration. Practice alone at home several times.
2. Do your demonstration for a friend as homework, or in class with a classmate.
3. Ask a partner to give you feedback on your performance using the feedback form on page 317, Appendix 2.

C. Give your demonstration to your class. Your teacher will give you feedback.

D. You may have the opportunity to do your demonstration for a group in the community. Look at the feedback your teacher gave you, and try to improve your demonstration.

Activity 2: Learn and share about American culture

Are you curious to learn how to do something "American" ? Take this chance to interview an American and find out how to do something that you are interested in.

Directions

A. Ask an American how to:

celebrate Christmas or other holidays

carve a Jack-o'-lantern for Halloween

color Easter eggs

celebrate an American-style wedding

go to a prom

make Christmas cookies

prepare a Thanksgiving dinner

greet people: older, younger, male, female

be a "good" guest when you do a home-stay

sing a traditional song

talk to a policeman about speeding

make a hamburger, banana split, or other American food

have a pizza delivered

buy a used car

talk to a landlord about problems with the apartment

let an American know you're interested in dating him or her

To begin the interview, you could say:
"Excuse me, could you explain to me how to _____ ? I've always been curious about it, and I'd like to teach my classmates about it."

B. After the interview, your teacher may ask you to share what you learned from your interview by doing a demonstration for your classmates, or by writing down what you learned as part of a handbook on American culture made by the class.

Activity 3: Keep an oral journal

On audiocassette, explain the skill you learned during your interview. Remember to do the following:

_____ talk for 3 to 5 minutes

_____ introduce the topic

_____ give background information

_____ use step-by-step language

_____ explain new vocabulary

_____ close your explanation

Activity 4: Evaluate your work

Directions

After your demonstration, give an oral report to the class, or a partner, about your experience. The following form is an example of an oral report you can give. Your teacher may ask you to record your oral report on an audiocassette as part of your oral journal.

I gave a demonstration on _____ _____

to _____. I felt _____

about giving demonstrations before I started this chapter. During my

demonstration I felt _____ ,

because _____ _____ .

What I liked best about doing demonstrations was _____

_____ .

One problem I had was _____

_____ .

In conclusion, I feel like I have learned _____

_____ .

But I feel like I still need to _____

_____ .

CHAPTER SIX

GIVING SHORT SPEECHES

In this chapter you will learn how to:

- organize a speech
- speak so that you are understood
- use appropriate body language
- coach your classmates

RHYTHM PRACTICE

In this chant, you will practice the pronunciation of expressions used to give a speech and coach your classmates on their speeches.

Directions

1. Listen to the chant.
2. Repeat after your teacher.
3. Practice the chant several times with a partner. One of you reads A, and the other reads B.

A: HelLO, everyBODy.
Did you ever GIVE a SPEECH?
ToDAY I'll tell you HOW.
It's EASier than you THINK.

B: Speak UP, slow DOWN,
Look aROUND, reLAX!
Speak UP, slow DOWN,
Look aROUND, reLAX!

A: FIRST of all, prePARE.
THEN try SPEAKing SLOW.
NEXT, look at your AUdience.
And FINally, speak LOUD.

B: Speak UP, slow DOWN,
Look aROUND, reLAX!
Speak UP, slow DOWN,
Look aROUND, reLAX!

A: In conCLUSion, please
ReMEMber this toDAY,
SPEAK so we can underSTAND
ALL you have to SAY.

B: You did GREAT.
Try aGAIN.
And slow DOWN and reLAX!
Speak UP, slow DOWN,
Look aROUND, reLAX!

MODEL CONVERSATION

Directions

1. Read the conversation silently.
2. Listen to the conversation.
3. Read it out loud with a partner, changing roles each time.
4. Answer the questions that follow.

(Toshi is rehearsing his speech in Ms. Ward's office. The teacher is stopping him to give him advice.)

Toshi: *(Speaking softly)* Have you ever had to take a test that would determine your entire future? What kind of job you could get? How much money you would make? Your status in society for the rest of your life? Every year, millions of young people in East Asia must take such a test. In just one or two days, our fates are decided.

Ms. Ward: Could you speak more loudly, please?

Toshi: Okay. *(Speaking loudly, but only looking at his paper).* Today I will talk about university entrance examinations. I feel strongly that university entrance examinations such as we have in Japan should be abolished; in other words, they should not exist anymore.

Ms. Ward: That's great, but you're looking down at your paper the whole time. Would you look up, please?

Toshi: But I can't remember what I'm going to say.

Ms. Ward: If you forget, just look down at your notes quickly, and then look up and continue speaking.

Toshi: Okay, I'll try. *(Speaking quickly and making eye contact).* For one thing, the exams are too difficult and high school students in Japan have to spend all their time studying for them. As an example, a government survey showed that last year high school seniors spent an average of six hours a day studying for college entrance exams.

Ms. Ward: I'm sorry, but you're going so fast I'm afraid no one will be able to follow you. Could you speak more slowly?

Toshi: Yes. *(Speaking more slowly.)* For another thing, we are forced to learn a lot of useless information for the exams that we will never need again. For example, we must memorize the names of authors and the dates of historic events.

And finally, the exams do not measure the true academic ability of students. In other words, someone might do very good work in class, but not be able to pass the entrance exam.

In conclusion, the exams do not do what they are supposed to do, and they waste our precious youth. I believe, therefore, that we should get rid of, or stop using, the exams, and we should think of a better system to take their place.

Ms. Ward: That was better that time. You did an especially good job explaining vocabulary. Let's try it again.

Questions on the Model Conversation:

1. How does the teacher interrupt Toshi politely?

2. What expressions does the teacher use to tell him to look at the audience and speak slowly and loudly?

3. Does Toshi explain vocabulary during the speech, before the speech, or after the speech?

4. Underline the expressions Toshi uses to:

   a. introduce his topic

   b. get the audience's attention

   c. state his opinion about his topic

   d. give reasons and examples

   e. state his conclusion

   f. explain vocabulary

5. Listen to your instructor read the speech again. Mark with a slash each place where she pauses. Why does she choose to pause there? Why is it easier to understand her speech if she pauses?

SECTION 1: DELIVERING A SPEECH

> A "speech" can be anything from saying a few unprepared words in front of a small group of people, to a formal address to an audience of thousands. But whenever you speak in public, how you deliver your message is as important as what you say. In this chapter, you will practice the basics of giving an oral presentation so that people can clearly understand you.

Preview Questions

1. You read the class a short report. No one claps when you finish. Later your friend tells you, "It sounded interesting, but I didn't understand a word you said." What are some reasons the class might not have understood you?

2. You have just started a new part-time job and have to introduce yourself at a meeting to the other ten employees. You know that your pronunciation is not perfect. How can you speak so that everyone can more easily understand you?

Overview 1

Directions

1. Repeat the phrases after your teacher, making notes about intonation and stress.
2. Find some of these expressions in the Model Conversation on pages 119 and 120 and underline them.
3. Try to think of more expressions to add to the Overview.

Coaching someone on their voice

1. Could you speak more loudly (slowly, clearly) please?

2. It's hard to hear you. Could you (speak up)?

3. You're speaking very quickly. Try to slow down.

4. I think it would be better if (you paused a little after each main idea).

5. Could you try to (say each word clearly)?

6. _____

7. _____

Coaching someone on their eye contact and posture

1. Would you (look up please)?
2. Why don't you try (looking around at the audience)?
3. Would you try to (make eye contact)?
4. Could you (hold your head up)?
5. Remember to (stand up straight).
6. _____
7. _____

Practice 1.1: Coach your instructor

Directions

Your instructor will give a two-minute speech. She or he will try on purpose to do a very bad job delivering the speech. Interrupt your teacher politely to coach her or him on her or his voice, eye contact, and posture. (See Instructor's Manual for sample speech).

Practice 1.2: Give a two-minute speech

Directions

1. In a group of four or five, speak for two minutes on any topic (see suggestions below).
2. You have only one or two minutes to prepare.
3. You must keep talking the whole time. If you get stuck, repeat the last word that you said.
4. Try to remember to:

    _____ a. look around at each person in your group

    _____ b. speak loudly and clearly enough for everyone to hear you

    _____ c. emphasize important words

    _____ d. pause to give your audience time to think

    _____ e. sit up straight

5. While your group members are giving speeches, coach them using expressions from Overview 1 on pages 121 and 122.

Suggested topics:

1. my best friend
2. a memorable trip
3. a musician or music group I admire
4. my pet
5. a delicious food in my country
6. what I think of the weather here
7. my family
8. the most recent movie I saw
9. my favorite TV show
10. my favorite sport (to play or watch)
11. something I just bought
12. my favorite sports team
13. what I did today
14. my car
15. a book I read recently

SECTION 2: ORGANIZING A SPEECH

Preview Questions

1. What could you do to get your audience's attention at the beginning of your speech?

2. How does it help your audience understand your speech if you use transition words such as, "First, then, next"?

3. Why is it important to explain difficult vocabulary when you give a speech?

Overview 2

Directions

1. Repeat the phrases after your teacher, making notes about intonation and stress.
2. Find some of these expressions in the Model Conversation on pages 119 and 120 and underline them.
3. Try to think of more expressions to add to the Overview.

Getting the audience's attention

1. Have you ever (done something that you really regretted? Yes? Still, I guess none of you have ever gambled away all the money your mother sent you to buy a car).

2. Imagine you (suddenly get a mysterious letter in the mail. It tells you that you may have won a trip to Hawaii. Well, I received such a letter myself recently).

3. Did you know that (everyday dozens of babies are born with AIDS? And that most of these cases could have been prevented)?

4. The other day, (I was walking down the street and saw a man juggling on the corner. Across the street, a woman was playing the guitar. And further down the street, a theater group was putting on a play).

5. _____

6. _____

Introducing your topic

1. Today, I will talk about (why I will never go back to a casino).

2. I would like to talk about (my experience trying to collect my free trip).

3. I would like to tell you my opinion on (AIDS testing).

4. My topic today is (street performers).

5. _____

6. _____

Stating your thesis

1. This topic interests me because (I learned how even serious people can become reckless gamblers).

2. This topic should concern everyone because (nobody is sure if they can believe free offers).

3. I feel strongly that (everyone should be tested for AIDS before they get married).

4. I chose this topic because (I think street performances are the best entertainment around).

Stating main points

1. For one thing, (I made the mistake of drinking alcohol).
   For another thing, (I had too much confidence.)
   Finally, (I didn't know when to quit).

2. First of all, (I had to attend a sales presentation by the company offering the free trip).
   Then, (a salesman pressured me to buy a condominium in Hawaii).
   Last, (I did receive a coupon for a free trip to Hawaii. But in fact, I couldn't use it).

3. _____

4. _____

Giving examples

1. For example, (the casino offered me free drinks, and I ended up getting drunk.)

2. As an illustration of this, (the salesman actually told me I was stupid for not wanting to buy the condo).

3. As a case in point, (many states require people to get a blood test when they apply for their marriage license anyway).

4. For instance, (you can enjoy street performances for free).

5. _____

6. _____

Explaining vocabulary

1. In other words, (I won at first and then thought I would always win).

2. ("A condominium") is ("an apartment that you buy rather than rent").

3. This means that (you have to have a blood test before you can get married).

4. (You can watch the performacnes for free), or (at no cost).

5. _____

6. _____

Concluding your speech

1. In conclusion, (I learned that casinos can be dangerous. Don't go there, or you may end up like me, with no money. By the way, please don't tell this story to my mother).

2. To sum up, (free offers seem to be just another sales trick. If you accept such offers, you need to have a lot of patience and a lot of time).

3. I therefore believe (the government should require all people who get married and all pregnant mothers to be tested for AIDS. This could prevent the suffering of many babies and children).

4. In summary, (street performance is a way for amateurs to get an audience, and it is free and enjoyable for those who watch. I hope you'll go out this Sunday and take in some interesting entertainment on the street).

5. _____

6. _____

Practice 2

In this section, you will practice introducing, presenting the body of, and concluding eight different speeches on these topics:

Topic 1: "Why smoking cigarettes is a bad habit"

Topic 2: "How we can remember important birthdays"

Topic 3: "Why I love my pet rabbit"

Topic 4: "How falling in love with someone changes us"

Topic 5: "Why we should take care of our parents when they are old"

Topic 6: "What I would do with a million dollars"

Topic 7: "How to get a good grade in this class"

Topic 8: "Where to find a boyfriend or girlfriend"

You will practice the introductions, bodies, and conclusions of each speech separately first in Practices 2.1- 2.5. Then in Practice 2.6, you will combine all the sections of one of the speeches together and present it in front of the class.

Practice 2.1: Introduce a speech

Directions

A. Take turns using the best expression from "Getting the Audience's Attention," Overview 2, page 124, in the blanks. Work with one or more classmates.

1. **Topic:** why smoking cigarettes is a bad habit

   Do you know every cigarette you smoke shortens your life by 12 minutes?

2. **Topic:** how we can remember important birthdays

   Have you ever forgotten the birthday of someone you love?

3. **Topic:** why I love my pet rabbit

   You are having a very bad day. But you are still happy because when you go home, your very best friend is there.

4. **Topic:** how falling in love with someone changes us

Have you ever fallen in love with someone? I know I have.

5. **Topic:** why we should take care of our parents when they are old

The other day, I passed an old man on a park bench. It seems he was living in the park, and he was just my father's age.

6. **Topic:** what I would do with a million dollars

Imagine you get an envelope in the mail. You open it and it says you have just won one million dollars.

B. Take turns using a variety of expressions from "Introducing your topic" in Overview 2 on page 125 in the blanks.

1. *My topic today is* why smoking cigarettes is a bad habit.
2. *I would like to tell you* how we can remember important birthdays.
3. *Today, I will talk about* why I love my pet rabbit.
4. *I would like to talk about* how falling in love with someone changes us.
5. *I would like to tell you* why we should take care of our parents when they are old.
6. *My topic today is* what I would do with a million dollars.

C. Take turns using a variety of expressions from "Stating your thesis" in Overview 2 on page 125 in the blanks.

1. **Topic:** why smoking cigarettes is a bad habit

This topic interests me because, every day we are exposed to the effects of cigarettes whether we smoke or not.

2. **Topic:** how we can remember important birthdays

I chose this topic because I just forgot my mother's birthday last week, and I am in big trouble now.

3. **Topic:** why I love my pet rabbit

I feel strongly that I used to be quite homesick, but having a pet has helped me.

4. **Topic:** how falling in love with someone changes us

This topic interests me because we are all longing for love.

5. **Topic:** why we should take care of our parents when they are old

This topic should concern everyone because it is something we all will have to think about some day.

6. **Topic:** what I would do with a million dollars

I choose this topic because even though we may never get a million dollars, we all love to dream.

D. 1. Choose Topic 7 or Topic 8 and write your own introduction to a speech.
   2. Add expressions from Overview 2 on pages 124 and 125.
   3. Read your introduction out loud to your partner.

7. **Topic:** how to get a good grade in this class

   I. Introduction

     1. (Attention-getting question or story)

       Have you ever gotten a bad grade?

     2. (Your topic)

       Today, I will talk about how to get a good grade in this class.

     3. (Your thesis)

       I choose this topic because

8. **Topic:** where to find a girlfriend or boyfriend

   I. Introduction

     1. (Attention-getting question or story)

     2. (Your topic)

     3. (Your thesis)

Practice 2.2: Present the body of a speech

> In the body, you support your thesis about your topic with main points and examples.

Directions

A. Take turns using a variety of expressions from "Stating main points" in Overview 2 on page 125 in the blanks.

1. **Topic:** why smoking cigarettes is a bad habit

   a. _For one thing_ , cigarette smoking is expensive.

   b. _For another thing_ it gives you cancer.

   c. _Finally_ , it gives cancer to the people around you.

2. **Topic:** how we can remember important birthdays

   a. _First of all_ , we can write them down.

   b. _Then_ , we can connect them in our minds with another important event.

   c. _Last_ , we can ask someone to remind us.

3. **Topic:** why I love my pet rabbit

   a. _For one thing_ , he's nice to pet.

   b. _For another thing_ he's easy to talk to.

   c. _Finally_ , he doesn't ask much of me.

4. **Topic:** how falling in love with someone changes us

   a. _First of all_ , we become nicer people.

   b. _Then_ , we care more about our appearance.

   c. _Last_ , we have more energy.

5. **Topic:** why we should take care of our parents when they are old

   a. _For one thing_ , our parents gave us everything.

   b. _Then_ , our parents will need our help some day

   c. _Last_ , our children can learn from their grandparents.

6. **Topic:** what I would do with a million dollars

    a. _First of all_ , I would take a trip around the world.

    b. _Then_ , I would pay off all my debts.

    c. _Last,_ , I would donate the rest to charity.

B. Take turns giving examples for the main points of each speech. Use a variety of expressions from "Giving examples," Overview 2 on page 126.

1. **Topic:** why smoking cigarettes is a bad habit

    a. Cigarette smoking is expensive.
    For example , one pack now costs $ _4_ .

    b. It gives you cancer.
    As an illustration of this , smoking has been proven to cause lung cancer.

    c. It gives cancer to the people around you.
    As a case in point , people who live with smokers have twice as high a risk of getting cancer as people who don't.

2. **Topic:** how we can remember important birthdays

    a. We can write them down.
    For example , every time we buy a new calender we can copy people's birthdays from our old calendar.

    b. We can connect them in our minds with another important event.
    As an illustration of this , my sister's birthday is easy to remember because it is on Valentine's Day.

    c. We can ask someone to remind us.
    For instance , my mother is very good at remembering birthdays, so usually I ask her to remind me.

3. **Topic:** why I love my pet rabbit

    a. He's fun to pet.

    As _acase in point_ , his fur is warm and soft.

    b. He's easy to talk to.

    As _an illustration of this_ , he seems to understand my English perfectly.

    c. He doesn't ask much of me.

    For instance , just a carrot makes him happy.

4. **Topic:** how falling in love with someone changes us

    a. We become nicer people.

    For example I'm so happy to be with my boyfriend/girlfriend that I am kinder to others.

    b. We care more about our appearance.

    As _an illustration_ , we dress up because we hope the one we love will tell us, "You look great."

    c. We have more energy.

    As _a case inpoint_ , since I fell in love I have gotten even more interested in studying and trying new sports.

5. **Topic:** why we should take care of our parents when they are old

    a. Our parents gave us everything.

    For example , our parents gave us life and raised us.

    b. Our parents will need us someday.

    As _a case inpoint_ , we can care for them when they are sick.

    c. Our children can learn from their grandparents.

    For instance , our parents can tell our children about the old days.

6. **Topic:** what I would do with a million dollars

   a. I would take a trip around the world.

     For example , I would visit the Middle East and Africa.

   b. I would pay off all my debts.

     As a case in point , I would pay off my credit cards and my student loan.

   c. I would donate the rest to charity.

     For example , I would like to give money to groups that help fight poverty.

C. 1. Continue with the topic you chose in part D of Practice 2.1, on page 129. Write the body of the speech.
  2. First write your topic, main points and examples.
  3. Then add expressions from Overview 2 on pages 125 and 126.
  4. Read the body out loud to your partner.

  1. **Topic:** *I would like to talk about my pets.*

    II. Body

     A. (First main point) *I have 2 puppies.*

      1. (Example) *their name are "thunder" and "Valentine."*

     B. (Second main point) *Puppies are Loveable,*

      1. (Example) *For example, they are small and easy to hold.*

     C. (Third main point) *I play with them.*

      1. (Example) *throw ball, jogging, jump, 2 legs walk.*

Practice 2.3: Conclude your speech

> In the conclusion, you can make a suggestion or prediction, and summarize your opinion in different words.

Directions

A. Take turns with a partner reading the conclusions below out loud. Use a variety of expressions from "Concluding your speech," Overview 2 on page 126.

1. **Topic:** why cigarette smoking is a bad habit

   _____ , people who smoke should try to quit. It is not just a personal choice to smoke. Smoking harms innocent people around you. If you can't quit by yourself, please ask for help from a doctor today.

2. **Topic:** how we can remember important birthdays

   _____ , we should try to remember people's birthdays because if we don't, we will hurt their feelings. I'm going to try my own advice and see if I can remember my mother's birthday next year.

3. **Topic:** why I love my pet rabbit

   _____ , some of you might think that only dogs can be man's best friend. Or you might think that a rabbit would make a delicious stew. But if you are looking for a small pet that will understand you, and that you can keep even in an apartment, please think about a rabbit. You might find it is the ideal pet for you, too.

4. **Topic:** how falling in love with someone changes us

   _____ , falling in love brings out the best in us. We become more grown up and responsible, thanks to love. I therefore hope that everyone can fall in love.

5.   **Topic:** why we should take care of our parents when they are old

_____ , old people should be living with their children, and not in nursing homes or on the street. Please start planning for your and your parents' future today.

6.   **Topic:** what I would do with a million dollars

_____ , winning a million dollars would allow me to do something for myself and also for others. But even if I don't win a million dollars, it's good to have dreams. And I hope I can still make my dreams come true, although it may be a little at a time.

B.   1.   Write a conclusion to the speech you worked on in part D of Practice 2.1, on page 129 and part C of Practice 2.2, on page 133.
     2.   Use an expression from Overview 2 on page 126 as you make your conclusion.
     3.   Remember to make a suggestion or prediction and to summarize your opinion.

1.   **Topic:** _Why smoking cigarettes is a bad habit._

III. Conclusion _Smoking cigarettes isn't good._

     A. Summary of your opinion

_____

_____

_____

     B. Suggestion or prediction

_____

_____

_____

Practice 2.4: Explain vocabulary

Before you give a speech, you should prepare to explain the meaning of any vocabulary that your audience might not know. Write the explanations into the speeches.

Directions

A. Take turns using expressions from Overview 2 on page 126 to explain the following vocabulary from the speeches in Practices 2.1 to 2.4.

1. a risk of getting cancer = a danger of getting cancer
2. hurt their feelings = make them feel bad
3. stew = a thick soup
4. grown up = like an adult
5. nursing home = a place where people live who cannot take care of themselves
6. donate the rest to charity = give the rest to someone who needs it

B. 1. Read through the speech you wrote in Practices 2.1 to 2.4 about "how to get a good grade in this class" or "where to find a boyfriend or girlfriend."
   2. Circle any vocabulary or expressions in your speech that your classmates might not understand.
   3. Write in an explanation of the words, using an expression from Overview 2 on page 126.

Practice 2.5: Deliver your practice speech

Directions

A. On another piece of paper, combine the introduction, body, and conclusion of one of the six speeches you just practiced in Practices 2.1 to 2.4, Topics 1 through 6. Deliver it in front of a small group or the class.

B. In the outline that follows, make notes on the speech you composed in Practices 2.1 to 2.4 about "how to get a good grade" or "where to find a boyfriend or girlfriend." Be sure to explain any difficult words. Then deliver your speech to the class or your small group.

I. Introduction

    A. (Attention-getting questions or story)

    B. (Topic)

    C. (Why important)

II. Body

    A. (First main reason or point)

        1. (First example or fact)

    B. (Second main reason or point)

        1. (Second example or fact)

    C. (Third main reason or point)

        1. (Third example or fact)

III. Conclusion

    A. (Summary or prediction)

    B. (Suggestion or opinion)

Practice 2.6: Listen to your classmates' speeches

Directions

1. As classmates present the speeches they prepared on Topics 7 and 8, make a simple outline of each speech on another piece of paper, like this:

Speaker's name:

Topic and thesis:

Main points:

1.

2.

3.

Conclusion:

---

2. If you can't complete the outline, ask your classmate to repeat all or part of the speech.

3. Your teacher will assign you a partner to give feedback to on their:

_____ speaking voice (speed, clarity, loudness)

_____ body language (posture, eye contact)

After all classmates have finished their speeches, give feedback to your partner on his or her speech. Use expressions from Overview 1 on pages 121 and 122.

REVIEW OF OVERVIEW EXPRESSIONS

Directions

1. Write one word in each of the blanks in the following conversation.
2. After you fill in all the blanks, compare your answers with those of a classmate.
3. Together, compare your answers with those in the Overviews on pages 121, 122, 124, 125, and 126.
4. Read the conversation together.

(Molly is helping Nita practice her speech.)

Nita: (*Speaking quickly.*) **1.** ___Have___ you ever wondered why you were spending years to learn English? Today I am going to **2.** ___talk___ about why English is a useful language to study. I chose this **3.** ___topic___ because I think if we realize how important English is, we will be more motivated to study it.

Molly: Excuse me, Nita, could you **4.** ___speak___ more slowly?

Nita: Okay. (*Speaking more slowly.*) For **5.** ___one___ thing, English is one of the most widely spoken languages in the world. As an **6.** ___illustration of this___, over 300 million people speak English as their native language, and over 100 million people speak it as a second language. The only language spoken by more people is Chinese. **7.** ___For___ another **8.** ___thing___ , English serves as a common language in the world for exchanging information. For **9.** ___example___ , most international conferences and events use English as the common language, and most computer data banks are in English. **10.** ___Lastly___ , English serves as a common language in the world for daily life. **11.** ___In___ other **12.** ___words___ , English can be understood in many countries when travelling and it is the national language for countries without a common native language, such as Ghana. In **13.** ___Summary___ , English may have started in England, but now it belongs to everyone. Even if we never live in England or the United States, it is still a useful tool for our lives.

Molly: That was great, Nita! Next time, **14.** ___you should___ to pause more after each main point.

Activity 1: Practice pausing and stressing key words

Directions

A. Listen to your teacher read the introduction to a speech. Circle the words that are stressed or said loudly. Put a slash where there is a pause. The first paragraph is done as an example.

1. Imagine you are looking up / at the night sky / The stars are coming out / and there are no clouds. / Suddenly / you see a silver disk hovering / or staying in the same place in the air, above you. / A silver antenna comes out of the disk / and points at you, / then goes back in. / In just a second, / the disk rises straight up into the sky / and disappears from sight.

Impossible, you say? / Well, / it happened to me. / My topic today is / UFOs / I believe UFOs exist. Let me tell you why.

2. First of all, UFOs have been sighted by thousands of people like myself. For example, even people who live in areas far away from civilization have reported the same hovering movement and antenna of flying saucers, or spaceships, that I saw. These are people who never read the news or watch TV.

3. Then, if UFOs did not exist, why would the U.S. government spend so much money to study them? We know for example that the U.S. Air Force has a special unit that investigates, or checks out stories of, UFOs.

4. And last, there is evidence that aliens have been visiting the earth since ancient times. As an example, drawings and statues found in caves, or holes in mountains, show beings with large heads, large eyes, no hair, and small bodies that match modern descriptions of aliens.

5. In conclusion, thousands of people throughout history have seen UFOs and even met creatures from other planets. I myself have seen a flying saucer with my own eyes. Just because we cannot explain these things does not mean they don't happen. So next time you are looking up at the night sky, who knows? Perhaps you will become a believer also.

B. 1. Read through the rest of the speech. Circle the words you think should be stressed and put a slash where you think there should be a pause.
   2. Read the sentences out loud for your teacher's feedback.

Activity 2: Make notecards

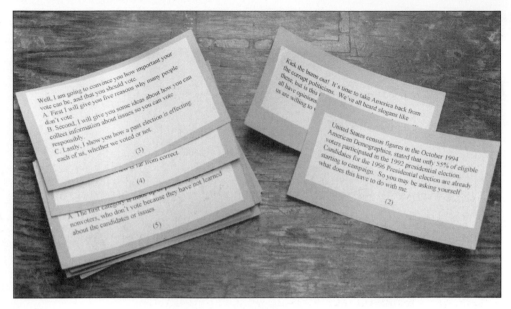

Before you give a speech, write down the key words and places to pause on notecards. Look at your notecards during your speech if you suddenly forget what you were going to say. You should still circle the words that you want to stress and put a slash where you want to pause on your notecards.

Example
Below is a notecard on the introduction to the speech on UFOs in Follow Up Activity 1.

NOTECARD 1

Attention-getting story

    Night sky/stars—no clouds/

    suddenly silver disk hovering (staying in same place)/

    silver antenna points/goes back/

    just second/rises straight up/disappears.

Thesis

    Impossible? Happened to me.

    Topic today: UFOs.

    UFOs exist.

    Why:

Directions

Make notecards for each paragraph of the speech on UFOs.

NOTECARD 2

First reason

Sighted by people / myself.

Example

in areas far away from civilisation

Same – hovering movement .
└ antenna of Flying saucers, spaceships → people who never read the news or watch TV.

NOTECARD 3

Second reason

U.S. government spend money to study them.

Example

U.S. Air force, check out Stories of UFO.

NOTECARD 4

Last reason

there is evidence – Aliens have been visiting the earth.

Example

drawing & statues in caves
holes in mountains.

NOTECARD 5

Conclusion

people throughout history have seen UFOs and Aliens.

Suggestion

you are looking up at the night sky.
may see it.

Activity 3: Give a short speech

Directions

A. Select one of the topics below for a five-minute speech, or think of your own topic.

1. why Americans drive junky cars
2. how living in a dormitory is different from living at home
3. how to avoid getting fat while in college
4. what college students do at parties
5. how my teachers now are different from teachers I had in high school
6. what I miss the most about my hometown
7. what the ideal romantic partner is like
8. what I would buy with a million dollars
9. the three things that shocked me in a foreign country
10. my dreams for the future
11. a holiday in my country
12. what my parents taught me
13. the best concert I ever went to
14. popular jokes in my native language
15. the three worst points of this town
16. the times when I get homesick
17. my most unusual friend
18. an important political event
19. who I think is the greatest world leader
20. why I think everyone should learn a foreign language
21. the three things I wish I had brought with me to this college
22. the three places I would like to see in the world.
23. my days on the (soccer, basketball, baseball, etc.) team
24. my secret hobby
25. the happiest day of my life (so far)

B. Write a draft of your speech. Remember to do the following:

Introduction

_____ greet the audience: say "good morning" or "good afternoon" at the start and "thank you for your attention" at the end.

_____ start with an interest-catching first sentence

_____ state your topic

_____ state your opinion of the topic (your thesis)

Support

_____ give main points that support your thesis

_____ follow each main point with an example or an explanation

Conclusion

_____ summarize or restate your opinion

_____ give a suggestion, or make a prediction

Vocabulary

_____ explain any difficult words during your speech

C. Practice your speech alone and with friends and classmates. Try giving your speech in front of the mirror and recording it on cassette tape. Remember to:

_____ Look around at the audience often—even the people at the sides or in the back of the room. If you must look at your notes, do so quickly, and then look up again as you speak.

_____ Stand up straight, and don't grip or lean on the podium. Keep your hands free and relaxed. Try to avoid making movements or gestures that will distract your audience.

_____ Speak loudly, and not too quickly. Mark the words you should stress and the places you should pause in your notes.

Activity 4: Give a speech based on an out-of-class interview

Directions

1. Interview several people outside of class about a topic that interests you.
2. Prepare a speech about the results of your interview.
3. Explain important vocabulary words during your speech.
4. Prepare questions about your speech for your classmates to discuss.

Example: "Drug Use in the U.S."

Do you think drugs are a problem in America? Today I will talk about what I learned by interviewing Americans on the topic of drug use, or taking illegal drugs. I think this is an important issue, because we hear so much about drug use in America even before we come here, and it makes many of us afraid.

I was surprised by three things during my interview. The first thing that surprised me was that not all Americans have used drugs. As an example, seven of the ten people I interviewed had never used marijuana.

The second surprising thing was that most of the Americans I interviewed called alcohol, or wine, beer, and liquor, a drug. In my country, we never think of alcohol as a drug, so this seemed very strange to me. In other words, the Americans seemed to think that alcohol caused many problems, maybe as many as drugs.

Finally, I was also surprised that five of the Americans I interviewed thought marijuana should be legalized, or not against the law. They thought it was no worse than alcohol. The other five Americans disagreed. They thought using marijuana started people using other drugs.

In conclusion, I learned many interesting things about how Americans feel about drugs. I learned that not all Americans use drugs, that alcohol is called a drug, and that Americans don't agree about marijuana. I also realized that in my country, drugs are not a problem, but maybe alcohol is. What do you think?

Discussion Questions

1. What did you think about drugs in America before you arrived? Has that changed?

2. What do you think about marijuana?

3. Do you think alcohol is a drug? Why or why not?

Activity 5: Observe a speech

Directions

A. Listen to someone who is not in your class give a speech in English. On another piece of paper, take notes on the:

_____ purpose of the speech (where given? why?)

_____ topic

_____ speaker's name (if known)

_____ length of speech

_____ main points

_____ conclusion

_____ anything about the delivery that was the same as what you learned in class

_____ anything about the delivery that was different from what you learned in class

_____ any new ideas about giving speeches that you got

Ideas for opportunities to observe speeches:

1. a speech communication or other college class where students give oral presentations (by special permission of the instructor)

2. a guest speaker invited to your class to give a short speech on a topic of interest or controversy

3. a presentation by a visiting scholar on campus that is open to the public

4. a thesis defense by a graduate student open to the student body

5. speeches given by another class in your English program

6. a local speech contest

7. videotapes of speeches by well-known leaders, such as Martin Luther King, Jr., Malcom X, John F. Kennedy, Mother Teresa, and so on (may be available in your school or civic library)

B. Record a report of the speech you observed on audiocassette as an oral journal activity. Remember to:

_____ include important or interesting information from your notes

_____ speak for 3 to 5 minutes

Activity 6: Evaluate your work

Directions

Answer the following questions about the speech you gave in Follow Up Activity 3 and be prepared to discuss them with your teacher.

1. Was this a topic you were truly interested in and excited to tell the class about?

2. Preparation (give yourself from 1 to 5 points, based on how much energy and time you put into these):

	little effort				great effort
a. written draft of speech	1	2	3	4	5
b. outline or notes to refer to during speech	1	2	3	4	5
c. explanations of vocabulary	1	2	3	4	5
d. practiced alone or with friends	1	2	3	4	5
e. practiced pronunciation of difficult words	1	2	3	4	5

3. Delivery (give yourself from 1 to 5 points, based on how well you remembered to do these during your speech)

	forgot				remembered
a. looked around at the class	1	2	3	4	5
b. spoke slowly, clearly, paused	1	2	3	4	5
c. spoke loudly, passionately, stressed key words	1	2	3	4	5
d. stood up straight, relaxed posture	1	2	3	4	5
e. remembered important points	1	2	3	4	5

Other comments on your speech:

CHAPTER SEVEN

DISCUSSING IN SMALL GROUPS

In this section you will learn how to:

- express your opinion
- clarify someone else's opinion
- agree and disagree politely
- facilitate a discussion

RHYTHM PRACTICE

In this chant, you will be introduced to some of the expressions you can use in a discussion.

Directions

1. Listen to the chant.
2. Repeat after your teacher.
3. Practice the chant several times with a partner. One of you reads A, and the other reads B. Then change parts.

A: What do you THINK?

B: It's a GOOD IDEA.
What do YOU think?

A: Hmm . . .
I SEE what you MEAN.
I SEE what you MEAN.
I SEE what you MEAN, but . . .

B: But WHAT?
But WHAT?
But . . .
WHAT?

But WHAT?
But WHAT?
But . . .
WHAT?

A: You've got a GOOD POINT,
A VERY good point,
An EXCELLENT point, but . . .

B: But WHAT?
But WHAT?
But . . .
WHAT?

But WHAT?
But WHAT?
But . . .
WHAT?

A: But . . .
But . . .
But . . .
Oh, TIME'S UP!
TOO bad, TOO bad,
TIME IS UP.

MODEL CONVERSATION

Directions

1. Read the conversation silently.
2. Listen to the model conversation.
3. Read it out loud four times in a group of four, changing parts each time.
4. Answer the questions that follow.

(These students are discussing the best way to learn English in a small group. Two of the students are behaving badly, but the leader does a good job of controlling the discussion.)

Lee: We're supposed to come up with the best way to learn English. Would anyone like to start?

Molly: Please don't ask me. I have absolutely no idea.

Nita: Molly, you were supposed to prepare your opinion as homework. What's the matter with you? Don't you care if we get a good grade?

Molly: Oh, shut up.

Lee: I think we're getting off the subject. Maybe I'll start. I think the best way to learn English is to watch TV. I watch the news every night and my listening comprehension has really improved! How about you, Carlos? What's your opinion?

Carlos: Well, I'm afraid I disagree with you.

Molly: Oh? Well, what do you think is the best way to learn English?

Carlos: In my opinion, having an American girlfriend is the best way to learn English! You can practice for hours and you really care what you're talking about together.

Nita: So what you're saying is you'd rather fool around than study English.

Molly: Hah, hah, very funny.

Lee: Let's try to stick to the topic of this discussion and avoid personal comments. It seems to me that we are all saying that the best way to learn English is to practice a lot. And it's also important to find something in English you are really interested in, whether it's the news or a relationship. Does everyone agree?

All: Yeah.

Lee: Molly, would you give the report to the class, then?

Molly: Okay. (*Stands up and reports to class*). "In our group, we didn't [2] really have any idea about how to learn English."

Nita: [3] Molly, you idiot! That's not what we said at all.

Molly: Shut up, Nita.

Questions on the Model Conversation:

1. Who do you think is the leader of the discussion? Why? *Lee*

2. Molly seems to be annoying her group members—why? Give examples. *Molly*

3. Nita also disrupts the discussion—how does she do this? *Blame. Molly*

4. What expressions does Carlos use to express his opinion politely? *In my opinion*

5. What expressions does Lee use to: *suppose to*
   - open the discussion? *we're* *would anyone like to start?*
   - get everyone to talk?
   - keep everyone on task? *we're getting off the subject*
   - close the discussion? *does everyone agree*

SECTION 1: EXPRESSING YOUR OPINION

Preview Questions

1. When was the last time you filled out a questionnaire or took part in an opinion poll or survey? What was the topic?

2. When was the last time you discussed something with someone? Who was it? What did you talk about?

3. Why is it useful or interesting to find out what other people think?

4. Why do you think teachers often ask students to discuss their opinions in class (rather than just listen to a lecture)?

Overview 1

Directions

1. Repeat the phrases after your teacher, making notes about intonation and stress.
2. Find some of these expressions in the Model Conversation on pages 152 and 153 and underline them.
3. Try to think of more expressions to add to the Overview.

Asking opinions

1. What do you think (is the best way to learn English)?

2. Do you think (students should speak their native language in class)?

3. How do you feel about (living with a homestay family)?

4. Do you agree or disagree that (reading novels helps improve your English)?

5. _____

6. _____

Expressing opinions

1. I think that (making an American girlfriend is the best way to improve your English).

2. In my opinion, (listening to the news on TV is the best way to improve your English).

3. I believe that (the best way to improve your English is to master English grammar).

4. It seems to me that (you should start by perfecting your pronunciation).

5. _____

6. _____

Practice 1.1: Conduct an opinion poll

In these exercises, you will conduct an opinion poll of your classmates about one of the topics below or another topic your teacher assigns you.

Topics

1. our school
2. an ideal job
3. a popular music group
4. a recent movie
5. an exciting sport
6. a way to stay healthy
7. a place to travel
8. arranged marriages
9. househusbands
10. drinking alcohol

Directions

A. Use expressions from Overview 1, page 154 to ask your classmates for their opinions on your topic.

Example of a question on topic #1:

What do you think is the best point of this school?

Your question

_____

_____

B. Make a simple chart on another piece of paper to use to record your classmates' answers while you are polling them. Turn in your results to your instructor in this format.

For example, if it is a Wh- question:

	Number of answers
1. What are the best points of this school?	
a. cafeteria	2
b. library	3
c. teachers	4
d. etc.	

If it is a yes-no question:

1. Should 18-year-olds drink alcohol?

Yes	Reasons
6 (people)	3—young people already drink anyway
	2—a little alcohol is not harmful
	1—18-year-olds in my country drink and it's no problem
No	
10 (people)	7—young people are not mature enough to handle it
	3—it will increase the number of traffic accidents
Other answers	
It depends on:	1—whether they are still in high school or not
	1—how much they drink

C. 1. Use expressions from Overview 1 to ask all your classmates for their opinion regarding your question.
   2. Record their answers on your chart.
   3. Then your classmates will ask you their questions.
   4. Use expressions from Overview 1 to express your opinion.

SECTION 2: AGREEING AND DISAGREEING

Preview Questions

1. Why is it helpful to be polite when you disagree with someone?

2. Sometimes you disagree with someone, then find out later you had misunderstood them. How can you avoid this?

3. Why is it better to also give reasons for your opinion, rather than just saying your opinion?

Overview 2

Directions

1. Repeat the phrases after your teacher, making notes about intonation and stress.
2. Find some of these expressions in the Model Conversation on pages 152 and 153 and underline them.
3. Try to think of more expressions to add to the Overview.

Agreeing

1. I think so, too.

2. That's right.

3. My answer is almost the same as (yours).

4. I agree with (you).

5. I feel the same way.

6. _____

Disagreeing politely

1. I agree with (you), but I also think (you're only seeing one side of the issue).

2. I'm afraid I disagree with (you).

3. I see what (you) mean, but (I think you can also practice English with host families and friends).

4. (You've) got a good point, but I have a slightly different opinion.

5. That's true, but (not everyone has a TV at home).

6. _____

Clarifying others' opinions

1. So what you're saying is that (watching movies is the best way to learn English).

2. In other words, (you think the most important thing is to improve your listening comprehension).

3. If I understand what you're saying correctly, then you think (you can remember vocabulary better if you study it before you sleep).

4. Let me get this straight. You mean that (we can learn a lot of English from getting a part-time job in the U.S.).

5. _____

6. _____

Rephrasing your opinion

1. That's not quite what I meant.

2. Let me try to explain again.

3. No, what I meant to say is (it's easier to practice English with someone we love).

4. No, what I mean is that (we can learn a lot of current vocabulary from the newspaper).

5. _____

6. _____

Practice 2.1: Agree and disagree

Directions

1. Make a group of three people and discuss the opinions below using expressions from Overview 2 on page 157.
2. Take turns being student A, B, and C.

   Student A expresses the statement as his or her opinion.
   Student B agrees with Student A, and gives a reason.
   Student C disagrees with Student B, and gives a reason.

Example

A:	It seems to me that (the best point of this school is the delicious cafeteria food).
B:	I feel the same way, because (the food is cheap).
C:	That's true, but (the food is usually really greasy).

1. The best point of this school is the cafeteria food.
2. The ideal job is being a professional gambler.
3. It's better to listen to classical music than popular music when you study.
4. Hollywood movies have too much violence and sex.
5. Soccer is the greatest sport in the world.
6. Going to bed early and getting up early is the best way to stay healthy.
7. The Middle East is the most exciting place to travel.
8. Arranged marriages are the best way to find a partner.
9. Househusbands are every woman's dream.
10. Alcohol is a dangerous drug.

Practice 2.2: Clarify and rephrase opinions

Directions

1. Take turns being student A and B.
2. Student A expresses an opinion about the topics below.
3. Student B clarifies Student A's opinion.
4. Student A agrees, or rephrases his or her original opinion.
5. Use expressions from Overview 2 on page 158.

Example

A:	In my opinion, (the best point of this school is the library. It's a great place to study).
B:	So what you're saying is that (it has a lot of books and journals for doing research).
A: *OR:*	That's right. No, what I mean is that (the library has really comfortable chairs. When I get tired of studying, I can take a nap there).

Topics

1. the best point of this school
2. the ideal job
3. the best music group
4. the best movie in the world
5. the most exciting sport

6. the best way to stay healthy
7. the most interesting place to travel
8. arranged marriages
9. househusbands
10. drinking alcohol

160 • • •

SECTION 3: FACILITATING A DISCUSSION

Preview Questions

1. Have you ever been part of a group or organization? (For example, a student council, club, or community group?) What kind of group was it? How often did you meet? What did you do at meetings?

2. What is the difference between a formal group discussion, such as a committee meeting or class discussion, and just chatting with a group of friends?

3. What should a discussion leader or facilitator do to help the discussion?

Overview 3

Directions

1. Repeat the phrases after your teacher, making notes about intonation and stress.
2. Find some of these expressions in the Model Conversation on pages 152 and 153 and underline them.
3. Try to think of more expressions to add to the Overview.

Opening the discussion

1. The topic of our discussion is (the best way to learn English). Would anyone like to start?

2. Today we have to decide (the best way to learn English). Shall we start by (brainstorming ideas)?

3. We're supposed to come up with suggestions for (the best way to learn English).

4. We all had some preparation to do for today's discussion. First of all, let's hear from (Nita) about (the results of her interview).

5. _____

6. _____

Keeping the group on task

1. I think we're getting off the subject.
2. Let's try to stick to the topic of this discussion.
3. Let's avoid personal comments.
4. Let's try to think of a compromise.
5. I think perhaps there's a misunderstanding here.
6. _____

Closing the discussion

1. It seems to me that we are all saying that (the best way to learn English is to practice a lot). Does everyone agree?
2. Let's see what we've come up with so far.
3. Would anyone like to add anything?
4. Does everyone agree (that we should take a vote)?
5. Time's up, so (let's stop here).
6. _____

Practice 3.1: Find solutions for common discussion problems

Directions

1. Make a group with four or more other students.
2. Decide how to solve the problems that follow.
3. Take turns facilitating the discussion of each problem. When it is your turn to facilitate, use the expressions from Overview 3 on pages 161 and 162 to open the discussion, keep the group on task, and close the discussion.
4. You will have five minutes to discuss each problem.

    a. Two members start arguing and become angry.

    b. Half the group wants to do one thing, and the other half wants to do another.

    c. The leader wants to decide everything by herself or himself.

    d. The group spends too long talking and never comes to a conclusion.

    e. The group agrees about something, but forgets the decision before the next meeting.

    f. One person almost never talks.

    g. The note-taker's summary to the class is different from what you actually said or decided.

Practice 3.2: Role-play a discussion problem and solution

Directions

1. In groups of four, role-play the situation below, using expressions from Overview 3 on pages 161 and 162.

Situation

You are trying to decide what kind of food to have at the class party. Students C and D get in an argument. Students A and B try to keep the group on task, reach a decision on which food to have, and close the discussion.

Characters

A = the leader; wants pizza

B = wants pizza or sushi

C = wants Chinese food or Mexican food and says bad things about pizza

D = wants pizza and gets angry at **C**

---

2. You will have about 5 minutes to perform your role-play for the class.

Practice 3.3: Have a longer discussion

Directions

1. Choose one of the topics from the opinion poll in Section 1 on page 155 to discuss in more depth.
2. Choose one person to lead the discussion and one person to take notes.
3. The note-taker should fill in the form on page 318, Appendix 2 with a summary of the main points of the discussion and turn it in to the teacher.
4. You will have about 20 minutes to discuss the topic.

REVIEW OF OVERVIEW EXPRESSIONS

Directions

1. Write one word in each of the blanks in the following conversation.
2. After you fill in all the blanks, compare your answers with those of a classmate.
3. Together, compare your answers with those in the Overviews on pages 154, 157, 158, 161, and 162.
4. Read the conversation once in a group of four.

(Molly, Carlos, Ricardo, and Nita are having a discussion to decide how to start a program for recycling garbage at their school.)

Molly: Today we are **1.** _____ to discuss the problem, "How can we start a recycling program at our school?" Would anyone like to **2.** _____ ?

Carlos: Sure, I will. I **3.** _____ the first thing we have to do is set up recycling bins in the cafeteria. You know, one container for glass, one for metal, one for paper, and one for other garbage.

Molly: That's a good **4.** _____ , but how can we make sure everyone will use the bins? Don't we need to tell everybody what we're doing first?

Ricardo: That's right. I **5.** _____ with Molly that we need to do some education first. In my **6.** _____ , we should start by making posters and having meetings.

Nita: So what you're **7.** _____ to say is that we need to tell everybody what recycling is first.

Ricardo: That's right, and also tell them why recycling is so important.

Molly: But won't it take a long time to organize meetings?

Carlos: Oh, by the way, Nita, are you going to see Michael tonight?

Molly: Excuse me, Carlos, but I think we're **8.** _____ off the subject. Nita, what do you **9.** _____ we should do first?

Nita: Well, it **10.** _____ to me that posters are easy to make. Why don't we put up posters and set up the bins right away, and then try to hold some meetings later?

Molly: Well, time's **11.** _____ . Does everyone **12.** _____ with Nita's suggestion of working on the bins and the posters right away?

Ricardo: Yeah, that sounds good.

Carlos: Great.

Activity 1: Have a formal discussion

Directions

A. 1. Bring some recent English-language newspapers to class.
   2. In small groups, look through the newspapers and try to brainstorm as many interesting discussion topics as you can.
   3. Try to think of more specific topics for each general topic you come up with. Examples of general and specific topics are given below to help you get started.

General topic: **Health**

  Specific topic: "new treatments for AIDS"

General topic: **Society**

  Specific topic: "gay marriages"

General topic: **Education**

  Specific topic: "financial aid for foreign students"

General topic: **Politics**

  Specific topic: "the role of the United Nations in peacekeeping"

General topic: **Sports**

  Specific topic: "professional athletes' salaries"

General topic: **Business**

  Specific topic: "free trade agreements"

Other:

B. Form groups of four or more people. By consensus and/or voting, choose one specific topic to discuss.

Your Topic

_____

_____

C. Try to put the topic in the form of a specific question. For example, if your topic is men and women's roles:

VAGUE QUESTION: "What do you think of men and women's roles?"

MORE SPECIFIC QUESTION: "Should men stay home and take care of small children?"

Your discussion question

_____

_____

D. With your small group, make questions about things you need to research before you can discuss the issue.

Examples

1. Are there societies in which men are responsible for taking care of children?
2. How many men in this society stay at home and care for children?
3. Is there anything men cannot do for small children?
4. Why aren't more men staying home and taking care of children now?
5. What are the good points of men, rather than women, caring for children?

Your questions

1. _____
2. _____
3. _____
4. _____
5. _____

E. Do one or more of the following as homework for the questions you came up with in part D.

    1. Interview someone using your questions, and take notes on their answers.
    2. Go to the library and research the answers to your questions.
    3. Conduct a survey or opinion poll of at least ten people on your discussion topic.
    4. Watch a news show or documentary to try to find answers to some of your questions.

F. 1. Discuss your topic with your small group, choosing one person to facilitate and one person to take notes.
    2. Ask a member of another group to watch you during the discussion and fill out the peer feedback form on page 319 of Appendix 2 for you.
    3. Read through the peer feedback form with the person who observed you and ask them to explain their comments.
    4. Get back together with your group and talk about how you can improve your discussion.

G. With your small group, hold a second discussion of your topic in front of the class. Your teacher will give you a grade or comments. Remember to:

_____ express your opinion

_____ agree and/or disagree, and say why

_____ help the group stay on task

If you are the leader, remember to:

_____ open the discussion

_____ close the discussion

Activity 2: Keep an oral journal

Directions

1. Look through a newspaper or watch the news on TV. Select a problem that you are interested in.
2. Record your personal opinion about it on an audiocassette tape (at least 3 to 5 minutes), and turn it in to your teacher for recorded comments.
3. Remember to say:

   _____ where you read or heard about the problem

   _____ what the problem is

   _____ what your opinion is about the problem

   _____ why you think so

   _____ other views you have heard about the problem

   _____ why you disagree with those views

Activity 3: Observe a discussion outside class

Directions

A. Watch people outside your class discussing their opinions. Even if you can't understand every word, try to get the gist of the discussion, and pay attention to the gestures, facial expressions, and tones of voice they use.

Ideas for ways to observe discussions

1. Ask permission to visit a college class where students discuss things in small groups.

2. Ask to join a group of students who are already talking in the school coffeeshop or cafeteria.

3. Watch a talk show on TV where people discuss controversial subjects.

4. If you live with an American family or share housing with Americans, ask them their opinions about a topic from class at dinner.

B. Write up a report about the discussion you observed, and turn it in to your teacher. Remember to describe:

_____ whom you observed

_____ where you observed them

_____ what they were discussing

_____ what the main points of agreement and/or disagreement were

_____ any expressions you heard them use to express their opinions, agree, disagree, and facilitate the discussion

_____ if they seemed calm or excited

_____ any gestures they used to express their feelings

Activity 4: Evaluate your work on this chapter

Directions

Circle your answers on this questionnaire.

Do you feel confident:

1. expressing your opinion?

    Yes   Somewhat   Not yet

2. clarifying someone's opinion?

    Yes   Somewhat   Not yet

3. agreeing?

    Yes   Somewhat   Not yet

4. disagreeing?

    Yes   Somewhat   Not yet

5. facilitating a discussion?

    Yes   Somewhat   Not yet

If you couldn't answer yes to all the questions, take some time to review the expressions in this chapter. Talk to your teacher and ask for more opportunities to practice the skills you are not sure of.

CHAPTER EIGHT

CONDUCTING A SUCCESSFUL INTERVIEW

In this chapter, you will learn how to:

- start an interview
- ask questions to hear opinions
- ask questions that encourage detailed answers
- create follow-up questions
- end the conversation

In this chant, you will be introduced to some expressions and strategies that can help you conduct a successful interview.

Directions

1. Listen to the chant.
2. Repeat after your teacher.
3. Practice the chant several times with a partner. One of you reads A, and the other reads B. Replace the words in parentheses to talk about yourselves.

A: HeLLO my name is (TOshi)
Can I DO an INterview?
Just ASK you a few QUEStions?
If IT's O.K. with YOU?

B: ALL right, go aHEAD, SURE, you BET
ALL right, go aHEAD, SURE, you BET.

A: WHAT do you THINK?
COULD you exPLAIN?
GIVE me an exAMPLE?
SAY that aGAIN?

B: I THINK so, MAYbe SO, NOT sure, GUESS so
I THINK so, MAYbe SO, NOT sure, GUESS so.

A: THANK you for your ANswers
THANK you for your TIME
ApPREciate your HELP
YOU've been very KIND.

B: NO problem, ANYtime, you're WELcome, pleasure's MINE
NO problem, ANYtime, you're WELcome, pleasure's MINE.

MODEL CONVERSATION

● ●

Directions

1. Read the conversation silently.
2. Listen to the model conversation.
3. Read it out loud twice with a classmate, changing roles each time.
4. Answer the questions that follow.

Hae-soo:	Excuse me, I'm studying English and need to do an interview for an assignment. May I ask you a few questions?
Woman:	I'm late for class, sorry. I've really got to run.
Hae-soo:	Oh, that's O.K. Thank you anyway.
Hae-soo:	Excuse me . . .
Man:	Yes?
Hae-soo:	I'm studying English and need to do an interview about homeless people for homework. May I ask you a few questions?
Man:	Sure.
Hae-soo:	Thanks. We've been talking about the issue of homeless people in this country. What do you think about this situation?
Man:	I think it's a real problem.
Hae-soo:	Why do you think that?
Man:	Well, there are more and more people living and sleeping on the streets. And shelters are really crowded.
Hae-soo:	I'm sorry, could you repeat that more slowly?
Man:	Oh yeah, sure. There are lots more people sleeping outside because they don't have homes. The shelters are crowded.
Hae-soo:	What does "shelter" mean?
Man:	Those are places to sleep organized by the city or religious groups.
Hae-soo:	Could you give me an example of what kind of people are homeless?
Man:	Well, of course there are some with drug or alcohol problems, but there are more and more homeless families now, too.
Hae-soo:	Families? Why do you think that is?

Man:	There's just not much cheap housing anymore. And a lot of the families just have the mom and kids and not much money.
Hae-soo:	What do you think should be done? 4
Man:	I really don't know. Maybe building more cheap housing and helping the homeless find jobs, if they can work.
Hae-soo:	What do you think about building more shelters?
Man:	Not effective.
Hae-soo:	I'd like to hear more about that. 4
Man:	Well, building them more shelters doesn't stop the problem. They are still homeless.
Hae-soo:	I see. Well, that's the end of my interview. Thanks so much for your help.
Man:	No problem. Glad to help.

Questions about the Model Conversation:

1. What phrases does Hae-soo use when she asks permission to interview people?

2. How does she explain about why she is doing the interview?

3. How did the woman say "no" to being interviewed by Hae-soo?

4. What phrases does Hae-soo use to encourage the man to give more information? How many can you find?

5. What did Hae-soo do when she couldn't understand?

6. How does she end the interview?

7. What did you think of Hae-soo's interview? Was it effective? Why or why not?

SECTION 1: STARTING AND ENDING THE INTERVIEW

Preview Questions

1. Have you ever done an interview? Have you ever been interviewed? Tell about your experience(s).

2. What is important to do before starting an interview?

3. How can you know if the person wants to be interviewed?

4. How should you start an interview? How should you end it?

Overview 1

Directions

1. Repeat the phrases after your teacher, making notes about intonation and stress.
2. Find some of these expressions in the Model Conversation on pages 173 and 174 and underline them.
3. Try to think of more expressions to add to the Overview.

Asking permission to do an interview

1. I'd like to interview you about (homeless people).

2. Can I ask you a few questions? It will only take (a few minutes).

3. May I ask you a few questions about (gun control)?

4. _____

5. _____

Giving or refusing permission to be interviewed

1. I wish I could, but I'm afraid I can't.

2. You bet. Go ahead.

3. I'm afraid (I've got to run).

4. _____

5. _____

Introducing your interview project

1. I need to do an interview about (your club) for my (homework).

2. We've been talking about (homeless people) in my (Sociology) class. I'm supposed to find out what opinions people have on (this issue).

3. I'm doing research for (a debate on gun control).

4. _____

5. _____

Ending the conversation

1. Well, that's the end of my interview. Thanks so much for your help.

2. Well, it's been nice interviewing you. I really appreciate your help.

3. Thank you for your help. You've been very kind.

4. _____

5. _____

Practice 1.1: Introduce your project/ask and give permission

Directions

A. Imagine your project is to find out about the International Club for an oral report you will present to your class. With a partner, take turns using various expressions from the Overview on pages 175 and 176 to:

1. introduce yourself and your project

2. ask permission to do an interview

B. Imagine you have called the International Club several times, but only get their answering machine. You decide to leave a message.

1. With a partner, discuss the following questions:

   a. How do you leave a message on an answering machine?

   b. What should you say first?

   c. Should you mention the day or time that you called?

   d. What things might you repeat?

   e. How would you end the message?

2. With a partner, role-play leaving a message to introduce yourself and your project. Use expressions from the Overview on pages 175 and 176 to introduce your project and to ask permission to do an interview. Remember to provide all important information so that someone can call you back.

Take turns reading the part of the answering machine:

Machine: "You have reached the International Club. Sorry no one is here to take your call, but if you leave your name and number after the beep, we will get back to you as soon as possible, thanks. . . . *Beep!*"

You:

Practice 1.2: Give and refuse permission, and end the conversation

Directions

The teacher will divide the class into two groups, A and B. Move to separate parts of the room. Read carefully the information on the paper the teacher gives you. *

Group A look here:

Each student in Group A is an "interviewer." Use various expressions from the Overview on pages 175 and 176 to do the interview.

1. Introduce yourself, and the project described on the paper your teacher gave you, to a member of Group B.

2. Ask permission to do an interview.

3. If your partner refuses, say "Well, thanks anyway" and continue to ask other members of Group B until someone agrees to be interviewed.

4. Sit down with your partner, and ask your partner the questions on your paper. Continue to discuss the topic until your teacher asks you to stop.

5. Use an expression from the Overview on page 176 to end your conversation. Give your paper back to the teacher and prepare to redo the activity as a member of Group B.

*Teacher: See Appendix 1, pages 302, 303, and 304 for a copy of the teacher's handout.

Group B look here:

Each student in Group B will be interviewed. When a member of Group A asks for permission to do an interview:

1. Listen carefully to the project your partner describes.

2. If the project is different from the project described on the paper your teacher gave you, use an expression from the Overview on page 175 to refuse permission.

3. If the project is the same as the project described on the paper your teacher gave you, use an expression from the Overview on page 175 to give permission to be interviewed.

4. When you find a partner with the same project, sit down together and answer the questions you are asked. Discuss the topic until your teacher asks you to stop.

5. Give your paper back to the teacher and prepare to redo the activity as a member of Group A.

SECTION 2: ASKING EFFECTIVE QUESTIONS

Preview Questions

1. You've tried interviewing people before, but the answers you received were only "Yes," "No," or "It depends." How could you get longer answers from the people you interview?

2. How can you make a person feel comfortable answering a question on a topic he or she may have strong feelings about?

3. How many questions do you need to prepare for an interview? Should you ask only those questions? Why or why not?

4. How can you remember the information you learn? Can you think of different methods?

Overview 2

Directions

1. Repeat the phrases after your teacher, making notes about intonation and stress.
2. Find some of these expressions in the Model Conversation on pages 173 and 174 and underline them.
3. Try to think of more expressions to add to the Overview.

Asking questions that encourage detailed answers

1. Could you tell me a little about (your club)?

2. Could you explain (what "the science fiction club" does)?

3. What do you know about (campus security)?

4. _____

5. _____

Asking questions to hear opinions

1. How do you feel about (gambling)?

2. What is your opinion on (the problems of the homeless)?

3. Do you think that (racism is a problem in the U.S. today)? Why or Why not?

4. What do you think should be done?

5. _____

6. _____

Practice 2.1: Ask questions for in-depth information

> One way to encourage your partner to talk more and give more in-depth information is to avoid asking questions that can be answered by a simple "yes" or "no." Use information questions that begin with words like "How" or "What," or phrases which ask for a summary.

Directions

Look at the questions below and change all yes/no questions to information questions. When you finish, you should have a list of ten effective questions to use in Practice 2.2B.

Example

(Poor)	Does your father have a business?
(Better)	What does your father do?
(Best)	Could you tell me a little about your father's job?

1. Does your mother have a job?

2. Is your hometown nice?

3. Are you living in an apartment near school?

4. Do you like to travel?

5. Did you belong to a club in high school?

6. Do you have a special hobby now?

7. Do you know what you want to do in the future?

8. Are you studying English to use in business someday?

9. Do you have a best friend?

10. Do you have a favorite movie?

Practice 2.2: Ask follow-up questions

> An interview needs to be flexible. When someone gives you an incomplete answer, an answer you don't understand, or an interesting answer that you'd like to hear more about, you can get more information by quickly thinking of a new question, called a follow-up question.

Directions

A. Write several follow-up questions that you could use after each of the following responses. Refer to the Overview on page 180 if you need help.

Example

"He's a businessman."

You: *I'd like to hear more about his job. Could you give me an example of a typical day for him?*

1. "My mother is a housewife."
You: _____

2. "It's a big city."
You: _____

3. "I live in an apartment."
You: _____

4. "I'd like to go to Egypt."
You: _____

5. "I belonged to the rugby team."

You: _____

_____

_____

6. "I like to read."

You: _____

_____

_____

7. "I want to own a business."

You: _____

_____

_____

8. "I want to become a translator."

You: _____

_____

_____

9. "Linda is my best friend."

You: _____

_____

_____

10. "'Witness' is my favorite movie."

You: _____

_____

_____

B. Interview a partner using the improved questions you prepared in Practice 2.1 on page 180. Try to ask at least two follow-up questions for each topic. Take turns asking questions.

C. Interview the teacher about the following topics. One student should begin by asking a question that encourages a detailed answer. Other students should use follow-up questions to encourage the teacher to continue talking on that subject.

Topics

1. the TOEFL examination

2. a local college

3. courses offered next session in your program

4. something else you'd like to know

Practice 2.3: Ask questions to hear opinions

To encourage a person to give you their true opinion, you need to ask impersonal, **un**biased questions. A biased question shows the interviewer's opinion or indicates how the person being interviewed is expected to respond. Questions that are too directly personal should be phrased more generally.

For example:

What do you think of that awful new sculpture on campus? (a biased question)

What do you think of the new sculpture on campus? (an unbiased question)

Do you like to get drunk often? (a too-personal question)

How do you feel about people getting drunk often? (an impersonal question)

Directions

A. 1. Look at the questions below and change questions that are too personal or biased into questions that allow the person to answer comfortably.
   2. Remember to change any YES/NO questions into questions that encourage detailed answers.

1. Do you think gun control is bad?

2. Why aren't men and women treated equally?

3. Old people should live with their children, shouldn't they?

4. In your opinion, why don't people try harder to avoid divorce?

5. Wouldn't you say homeless people are lazy?

6. Why is smoking in public places bad?

7. Would you have a child without getting married?

8. Should the drinking age be 18?

9. Have you ever used drugs?

10. Why shouldn't we re-elect the president?

B. 1. Interview a classmate using the improved questions you created in part A.
2. Remember to ask follow-up questions.
3. Take turns interviewing.

· ·

Directions

1. Write one word in each of the blanks in the following conversation.
2. After you fill in all the blanks, compare your answers with those of a classmate.
3. Together, compare your answers with those in the Overviews on pages 175, 176, 179, and 180.
4. Read the conversation together.

Sarah: Hi. Can I help you?

Sami: I hope so. My name is Sami Badri. I need to **1.** _____ an interview about the International Club. **2.** _____ I ask you **3.** _____ few questions?

Sarah: **4.** _____ bet. I'm Sarah, secretary for the club.

Sami: Nice to meet you, Sarah. So, could you **5.** _____ me a **6.** _____ about your club?

Sarah: Sure. Americans and international students are all welcome to join. We meet Monday evenings at 7:00 in the lounge upstairs. And we put on an international dinner.

Sami: I'd **7.** _____ to **8.** _____ more about the international dinner.

Sarah: Well, once a year, in May, we have entertainment followed by a big dinner with foods from different countries.

Sami: Could you **9.** _____ me an **10.** _____ of what you talk about at the Monday meetings?

Sarah: For example, some of us are experiencing culture shock and need to talk with other people in the same situation. Sometimes our meeting seems like a support group.

Sami: Could you **11.** _____ what a "support group" **12.** _____ ?

Sarah: It's a group of people who all have the same problem and want to talk about it and help each other out.

Sami: That's the **13.** _____ of **14.** _____ interview. I really **15.** _____ your help.

Sarah: You're welcome. And I hope to see you Monday!

Activity 1: Survey and interview your classmates

Directions

A. Choose one of the questions you rewrote in practice 2.3 on pages 183 and 184. Walk around the classroom interviewing as many of your classmates as possible. Remember to ask follow-up questions. Take notes on interesting opinions you hear.

B. Share the results of your survey with the class by summarizing the results orally.

Example

I interviewed _____ classmates with the following question: _____

_____ ?

Some/most people said _____

_____ ,

_____ ,

and others/no one thought _____ .

I think that _____

_____

_____ .

Activity 2: Role-play a television interview host

Directions

With a partner, prepare a 3 to 5 minute dialogue. Partner A should play the role of a famous television interview host. Partner B should be a character well known to the people in your class (a president or world leader? a famous person from the past? Mickey Mouse? A classmate or teacher?). Remember to:

_____ make your interview/role-play 3 to 5 minutes long.

_____ include expressions from the Overviews on pages 175, 176, 179, and 180.

_____ look at pages 51 and 52 for language to use when planning your role-play

_____ refer to the evaluation form in Chapter 3, Actvity 5, page 66 for hints on making a successful role-play.

Activity 3: Conduct an interview about a controversial issue

Directions

A. Prepare for your interview by doing each of the activities listed below:

_____ Select a controversial issue to interview English speakers about.

_____ Learn some information and vocabulary about your topic before the interview.

_____ Prepare questions that cannot be answered with a simple "yes" or "no."

_____ Prepare questions that accept any answer as "correct." Avoid "biased" questions or questions that are too directly personal.

_____ Make sure your questions are all focused on the same topic.

_____ Show your questions to your teacher to be checked.

_____ Practice pronouncing your questions clearly.

B. Using the interview you prepared in part A, interview at least four people who are not classmates. Remember to do the following:

_____ Introduce yourself and what you are doing. Explain how long you think the interview will take. Make sure it is a convenient time for the person you are interviewing.

_____ Ask the questions you prepared, but be flexible. Ask new follow-up questions when something you hear interests you.

_____ Ask people to repeat or explain when you don't understand.

_____ Take a few notes, but don't write out long sentences until after the interview is finished. Consider using a tape recorder.

_____ Thank the person you interviewed.

C. Prepare a short speech about your interview.

1. Think about your interview experience:

   a. What were some of the most interesting things you learned?

   b. What did it make you think about?

   c. What's your opinion now?

2. Organize your speech following the outline in Chapter 6, Activity 3B, "Giving a speech", on page 145. See page 146 for a sample speech.

Activity 4: Make an interview-based class newsletter

Directions

1. As a class, choose a theme for a newsletter your class will produce. Look at the list below for some suggestions.
2. Brainstorm different interview projects that would investigate the theme the class has chosen.
3. Assign each member of the class a different interview project.
4. Each member should do the interview, and write up a two-to-three paragraph report.
5. The class should collect all of the reports to be put together in a newsletter.

Possible themes for the newsletter

1. clubs and student organizations on campus

2. life stories of classmates

3. interviews with interesting local people in various professions

4. a survival handbook for new students

5. families in America

6. profiles of instructors

Activity 5: Keep an oral journal

Directions

On audiocassette, record the results of an interview you did in Activities 1, 3, or 4. Remember to:

_____ talk for 4 to 5 minutes

_____ speak naturally, without reading

_____ explain what you learned during the interview

_____ explain what surprised or interested you

_____ ask any questions you now have on that topic

Activity 6: Evaluate your work

Directions

How well did you prepare and conduct the interviews in this chapter?
Answer the questions in the chart below.

1.	I learned a little about my topic and the vocabulary I might hear before I did my interview(s).	YES	NO
2.	I prepared non-biased questions.	YES	NO
3.	I encouraged the person I interviewed to give in-depth questions by preparing information answers instead of "yes/no" questions.	YES	NO
4.	I avoided asking "too-personal" questions by asking them in a more general way.	YES	NO
5.	I took the time to practice my pronunciation of new vocabulary.	YES	NO
6.	I introduced my project clearly.	YES	NO
7.	I asked people to explain or repeat when I didn't understand.	YES	NO
8.	I asked the questions I had prepared, but asked new follow-up questions when I heard something interesting or unclear.	YES	NO
9.	I took a few notes, but didn't write out long sentences until later/or I used a tape recorder.	YES	NO
10.	I thanked the person whom I interviewed	YES	NO

If you answered "no" to any of these questions, speak to your teacher about ways to get more practice to improve those areas.

CHAPTER NINE

GETTING HELP AT THE LIBRARY

In this chapter you will practice speaking skills
to help you do research at the library.
You will learn how to:

- ask a librarian for help
- explain your purpose and needs
- explain how to do something
- make sure you understand

RHYTHM PRACTICE

In this chant, you will practice the pronunciation of expressions and vocabulary you will need as you speak with librarians and do research.

▦ **Directions**

1. Listen to the chant.
2. Repeat after your teacher.
3. Practice the chant several times with a partner. One of you reads part A, and the other reads part B. Read the chorus together.

A:	MIcrofiche, MIcrofilm, enCYcloPEdia
B:	MIcrofiche, MIcrofilm, enCYcloPEdia
Chorus:	MIcrofiche, MIcrofilm, enCYcloPEdia

A:	OVersize, OVernight, can I CHECK it OUT?
B:	OVersize, OVernight, can I CHECK it OUT?
Chorus:	OVersize, OVernight, can I CHECK it OUT?

A:	CHECK it out, LOOK it up, then you WRITE it DOWN.
B:	CHECK it out, LOOK it up, then you WRITE it DOWN.
Chorus:	CHECK it out, LOOK it up, then you WRITE it DOWN.

A:	MIcrofiche, MIcrofilm, enCYcloPEdia
B:	OVersize, OVernight, can I CHECK it OUT?
Chorus:	CHECK it out, LOOK it up, then you WRITE it DOWN.

Chorus:	MIcrofiche, MIcrofilm, enCYcloPEdia

Chorus:	OVersize, OVernight, can I CHECK it OUT?

Chorus:	CHECK it out, LOOK it up, then you WRITE it DOWN.

MODEL CONVERSATION

● ●

Directions

1. Read the conversation silently.
2. Listen to the model conversation.
3. Read it out loud twice with a classmate, changing parts each time.
4. Answer the questions that follow.

(Carlos is in the library. He needs to find information for a speech he wants to give about AIDS. He goes to the reference area and talks to a librarian.)

Carlos: Excuse me, could you tell me how to find some information on AIDS? I'm supposed to give a short speech about it next week, but I don't know where to start.

Librarian: Sure. Is this the first time you've done any research here?

Carlos: Yes. I'm learning English and need to find some easy-to-read information.

Librarian: Well, first you could start with an encyclopedia. It uses simple language and gives general information. It's a good place to start. Then, if you want to read some articles from magazines or newspapers, you should use the computer database.

Carlos: Excuse me, but what does "computer database" mean?

Librarian: Well, for example, you can use this computer to look for newspaper, journal, and magazine articles on your topic.

Carlos: Oh, I see. Could you tell me where to find the encyclopedias?

(After Carlos has looked at an encyclopedia, he returns to ask the librarian another question.)

Carlos: I'd like to look at some magazine articles now. Would you mind showing me how to use the computer?

Librarian: Just a second and I'll show you.

Carlos: That'd be great.

Librarian: First you type in the word you want the computer to search for. Sometimes there are so many articles that you need to chose a subtopic, like "AIDS and Children." If a title looks interesting, you can choose to look at the abstract.

Carlos: I'm afraid I don't know what an abstract is.

Librarian: It's a short paragraph about the article. You can read it and decide if that article is something you want to look at. It tells you where to look, too. If you want a copy on paper, push the <F4> key. When you are finished looking at the list, make sure you push the <F3> key to print out the abstracts.

Carlos: Let me make sure I understand. First I type in the name of my topic. The computer will give me a list, and I can choose the ones I want to print out by pushing the <F4> key.

Librarian: That's right. And if you want to print out the list you just need to hit the <F3> key. Don't worry, you'll learn as you go along.

Carlos: Thank you very much for your help.

Librarian: You're welcome. Let me know if you're having problems.

Questions on the Model Conversation:

1. How does Carlos ask the librarian for help? What different phrases does he use?

2. How does Carlos ask the librarian to demonstrate the use of the computer?

3. How does Carlos make sure he understood correctly?

4. Where should Carlos begin his research? Why?

5. What is a computer database? What can Carlos find on the library's computer? Can he find books there?

6. What is a subtopic? Why might Carlos need to use a "subtopic"?

7. What does Carlos do when the librarian uses words or expressions that he doesn't understand?

SECTION 1: ASKING FOR HELP

Preview Questions

1. You've never used the library on campus before, but now you need to write a paper on "global warming." You're not even sure what "global warming" is. What should you do?

2. You want to find a video of Martin Luther King, Jr. giving a speech. Would the library have any of his speeches on video? How can you find out?

3. You'd like to take home a newspaper article you found, but it is on microfilm. What can you do?

Overview 1

Directions

1. Repeat the phrases after your teacher, making notes about intonation and stress.
2. Find some of these expressions in the Model Conversation on pages 193 and 194 and underline them.
3. Try to think of more expressions to add to the Overview.

Explaining your purpose and needs

1. I need to (write a five-page research paper).

2. I'm supposed to (compare and contrast two famous people).

3. I'm trying to find (recent articles on racism).

4. I'm having trouble (using the computer).

5. _____

6. _____

Asking for help

1. Could you tell me (where to find the microfiche)?

2. I'm afraid I don't know (where to look up) information on (UFO's).

3. What is the best (reference book) to (use)?

4. _____

5. _____

Practice 1.1: Prepare vocabulary

Directions

In this exercise, you and your classmates will teach each other vocabulary that you will need to do research at the library.

1. Your teacher will hand you a card with a word on one side and its definition on the other.

2. Memorize the word and the definition. Ask your teacher for help if you need it.

3. Tape the card to your shirt. You are now the "expert" on that word and will explain it to your classmates.

4. When your teacher says "start," stand up and take turns with your classmates explaining your word and asking about the meaning of the words attached to their shirts.

5. Do not read their explanations, and don't show them your written explanation. Ask questions when you don't understand.

6. Take notes on the meaning of each word on the list below. Try to find the meanings of all the words on your list.

7. When you have finished the activity, you can check your notes by looking at Appendix 1, page 305.

(an) abstract_____

alphabetical order _____

(an) article _____

(an) author_____

(to be) overdue _____

(a) call number _____

card catalog _____

(to) check out _____

(a) computer search _____

Editorials On File _____

(an) encyclopedia _____

(a) fine _____

(an) index _____

(a) journal _____

(a) loan desk _____

(to) look up _____

(a) main menu _____

microfiche _____

microfilm _____

(a) periodical _____

(to) print out _____

reference area _____

(a) subject/topic _____

(a) subtopic _____

(a) title _____

(a) volume _____

Practice 1.2: Form polite questions

As you work through the following exercises, you will practice using polite questions. Review how the following questions change form when we add the more polite "Could you tell me."

Where **is** the microfiche?
Could you tell me where the microfiche **is**?
What **was** the name of that book?
Could you tell me what the name of that book **was**?
How **do you use** this machine?
Could you tell me how **you use** this machine?
Which button **did** you **push**?
Could you tell me which button you **pushed**?

Directions

With a partner, take turns asking and answering polite questions. Change the questions listed below and try to have a conversation like the following:

A sees: Where is the music library?

A says: "Could you tell me where the music library is?"

B answers: "It's over in the Performing Arts Center."

A	B
1. Where are the video tapes?	They're on the fifth floor.
2. What time does the library close?	At 10:00 PM week-nights.
3. Where can I find a call number beginning with a Q?	Q's are on the fourth floor.
4. How do I use the card catalog?	Let me show you.
5. Where is the Periodical Room?	It's through those doors.
6. Where can I find QT138.25?	It's right after QT138.2 on the shelf.

Practice 1.3: Complete a library guide

Directions

You and your partner are going to ask for and provide information concerning a library guide.

1. Student A should look at Library Guide A. Student B should look at Library Guide B. Do not look at your partner's guide!
2. Ask your partner polite questions to find the missing information on your guide. Refer to Practice 1.2 if you need help.
3. Fill in the missing information on your guide. When you finish, the two guides should have the same information.

Student A look here:

Guide To Wilson Library

LIBRARY HOURS:

Mon–Thurs	7:45 AM – **1.** _____
Friday	7:45 AM – 5:00 PM
Sat–Sun	**2.** _____ – 6:00 PM

SERVICE AREAS:

Card Catalog Information Desk	1 Central
Copy Center	**3.** _____
Microfilm/Microfiche	5 West
Reference and General Information	1 Central

CALL NUMBER LOCATIONS:

A	**4.** _____
B	5 West
C, D	2 East
E, F, G, H	**5.** _____

Student B look here:

Guide To Wilson Library

LIBRARY HOURS:

Mon-Thurs   7:45 AM –11:00 PM

Friday   **1.** _____ –5:00 PM

Sat-Sun   12 noon– **2.** _____

SERVICE AREAS:

Card Catalog Information Desk	**3.** _____
Copy Center	1 West
Microfilm/Microfiche	**4.** _____
Reference and General Information	1 Central

CALL NUMBER LOCATIONS:

A	Basement Central
B	**5.** _____
C, D	2 East
E, F, G, H	3 East

SECTION 2: LEARNING HOW TO DO RESEARCH

Preview Questions

1. You want to use the computer in the library to do research for your paper, but you don't know how to use it. Who can you ask for help? What would you say?

2. A librarian is explaining how to find the location of a magazine you need. He is talking quickly. What can you say to make sure you have understood him correctly?

Overview 2

Directions

1. Repeat the phrases after your teacher, making notes about intonation and stress.
2. Find some of these expressions in the Model Conversation on pages 193 and 194 and underline them.
3. Try to think of more expressions to add to the Overview.

Asking for a demonstration

1. Could you show me how to (use this machine)?

2. Would you mind showing me (how) to (do that)?

3. Can I watch you do it step by step?

4. _____

5. _____

Explaining how to do something

1. First you should (type in your topic).

2. Then it's a good idea to (narrow your topic).

3. If you want to (print it out), you need to (push here).

4. When you (are finished), make sure you (turn it off).

5. _____

6. _____

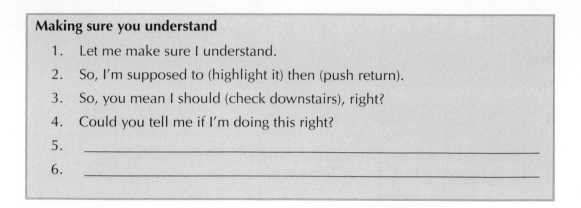

Making sure you understand

1. Let me make sure I understand.
2. So, I'm supposed to (highlight it) then (push return).
3. So, you mean I should (check downstairs), right?
4. Could you tell me if I'm doing this right?
5. _____
6. _____

Practice 2.1: Role-play asking for explanations in other situations

In this exercise, you will practice asking for information and making sure that you have understood, in situations other than in the library.

Directions

With your partner, invent a dialogue in which you explain how to do something and your partner checks to see if he or she has understood. Talk about one of the following situations.

1. asking and giving directions to a friend's house
2. finding out how to use a bank card
3. filling out an application to work in the cafeteria
4. (your ideas . . .)

Use the outline below:

A: (asks partner to show him or her how to . . .)

B: (agrees and explains directions step by step)

A: (checks that he or she has understood)

B: (confirms or corrects A's understanding)

A: (thanks B)

B: (ends conversation)

Practice 2.2: Ask for a demonstration and make sure you understand

Student A look here:

Directions

A. Use expressions from the Overview on pages 201 and 202 as you:
1. ask your partner how to use the copy center at the library.
2. listen carefully to the explanation your partner gives.
3. ask questions when you don't understand.
4. try to repeat the explanation when your partner has finished.
5. thank your partner.

B. Now switch roles. You will demonstrate for your partner how to use a machine to look at microfiche.

1. Use phrases from the Overview on pages 201 and 202 as you explain the following steps to your partner. Try to use gestures to demonstrate the steps.

HOW TO USE A MICROFICHE VIEWER

a. Switch the machine on here.

b. Pull out the glass plates, and slide your microfiche between them.

c. Use the knob on the side to focus.

d. Move the glass plates around and scan page numbers until you find the page you are looking for.

---

2. Listen as your partner repeats the directions. Repeat any part of your explanation that your partner hasn't understood.

Student B look here:

Directions

A. 1. Your partner will ask you how to use the copy center at the library. Use expressions from the Overview on pages 201 and 202 as you explain the following steps to your partner. Try to use gestures to demonstrate the steps.

HOW TO USE THE COPY CENTER

a. Collect all the materials you want to photocopy.

b. Go to the copy center window, and fill out one small paper for each group of pages that you want copied.

c. Be sure to write down the exact page numbers you want.

d. Ask the person working there when the copies will be ready.

e. Come back at that time, pay for your copies, and take them with you. The worker can return the books and magazines for you.

---

2. Listen as your partner repeats the directions. Repeat any part of your explanation that your partner hasn't understood.

B. Now switch roles. Use expressions from the Overview on pages 201 and 202 as you:
   1. ask your partner how to use a microfiche viewer.
   2. listen carefully to the explanation your partner gives.
   3. ask questions when you don't understand.
   4. when your partner finishes, try to repeat the explanation.
   5. thank your partner.

REVIEW OF OVERVIEW EXPRESSIONS

Directions

1. Write one word in each of the blanks in the following demonstration.
2. After you fill in all the blanks, compare your answers with those of a classmate.
3. Together, compare your answers with those in the Overviews on pages 195, 201, and 202.
4. Read the conversation together.

Toshi: Excuse me, I'm **1.** _____ trouble **2.** _____ the microfiche. **3.** _____ you tell me where to find it?

Librarian: The microfiche is kept in the files right against the wall over here.

Toshi: Thank you. (*He finds the microfiche he is looking for.*)

Toshi: Excuse me again, but I'm **4.** _____ I don't know how to use the microfiche reader. Would you mind **5.** _____ me **6.** _____ to use it?

Librarian: No, I'd be happy to. **7.** _____ you should turn on the machine with this switch. When you put in the microfiche, **8.** _____ sure that it is in this way. The knob underneath is used to focus; the one on the side is used to move around to different pages on the screen.

Toshi: So, you **9.** _____ I should use the knob underneath to focus and the one on the side to move from page to page, **10.** _____ ?

Librarian: That's right.

Toshi: Thank you very much for your help.

Librarian: You're welcome. Let me know if you need more help.

Activity 1: Create a student-led library tour

Directions

A. Working with a librarian

1. Your teacher will tell each student or pair of students to become the class expert(s) on one of the following research skills:

   a. how to use *Editorials on File* or *Facts on File*

   b. how to find out where different magazines are kept and how to find a specific magazine on the shelf

   c. how to use and photocopy information on microfiche

   d. how to use the card catalog to get a book's call number and how to find that book on the shelf

   e. how to use a computer to do research (2 students)

   f. how to use and photocopy from microfilm

   g. how to find and use audio and video resources

   h. how to find and use an encyclopedia

2. Go to the library and learn how to do the research skill which your teacher assigned you. Remember to:

   _____ ask a librarian for help

   _____ listen carefully and make sure you understand

   _____ use "censorship" (or another topic your teacher assigns) as the example you will use as you teach your classmates. Practice this example several times.

   _____ prepare another example that you can use when your classmates try out the research skill you have just presented

   _____ continue practicing until you feel confident in your new skill

B. Demonstrating a library research skill

1. At home, prepare what you will say when you demonstrate the library skill you have learned about in part A. Look at the guidelines in the box below as you prepare your demonstration. Your teacher will evaluate how well you follow these guidelines in your presentation.

> a. Be prepared—practice your demonstration before class.
>
> b. At the start of the presentation, tell your classmates exactly WHAT they will learn HOW TO DO.
>
> c. Speak loudly and demonstrate so that everyone can see.
>
> d. Check often to see if your classmates understand.
>
> e. Warn them about any parts that might be difficult.
>
> f. When you finish, have one or two classmates TRY TO DO IT WITH A NEW EXAMPLE. Make sure you prepare these examples ahead of time!
>
> g. Answer questions after your presentation and while your classmates are trying out the new skill.

2. As your classmates take you through the library and teach you the skill they have "mastered":

a. pay careful attention and take notes

b. ask questions

c. volunteer to try out the new skill during the demonstration

You will need to know how to use each of these resources in later activities.

Activity 2: Have a scavenger hunt at the library

Directions

In this activity, you will work with a partner to finish all of the tasks on the list below. You must stay with your partner at all times. You will need this list, some coins for the copy machine, a library card, and any notes you took during the library demonstrations done by your classmates.

The team who completes the list first, and follows all of the rules, WINS!

RULES

1. Be quiet!
2. No running.
3. Stay together.
4. Complete your list in the correct order (as assigned).
5. Put back any resources you use.

SCAVENGER LIST

1. Find a call number for a book about Tanzania.
2. Each of you make a photocopy of the front page of *The New York Times* newspaper from the day you were born.
3. Each of you photocopy the cover of *Time* magazine from the week that you were born.
4. Make a photocopy of something on microfiche.
5. Each of you print out the abstract for one recent article on your home country.
6. Each of you find a book about your home country.
7. Check out a book.
8. Find out the library hours on Sundays.
9. Write down the name and call number of one video tape kept at the library.

Activity 3: Do independent research

Directions

1. Choose a topic, or research the topic your teacher has assigned for a class debate, interview, or speech.
2. Look in a recent encyclopedia. Photocopy one page that talks about your topic.
3. Use a computer database to find a newspaper and a magazine article on your topic. Write down the name of the author, magazine, volume, date, and page numbers.
4. Using a computer database, print out two abstracts about articles you find on your topic.
5. Find the magazine and newspaper and make a photocopy of at least part of each article.
6. Check the card catalog for books on your topic. You do not need to check out the book, but please write down the name and call number.
7. Find out if there are any audiovisual resources on the topic, and note the titles.
8. Make a collection of your research to turn in to your teacher. Include everything on the checklist below:

_____ A specific topic
_____ A photocopy from the encyclopedia
_____ Two abstracts from the database
_____ Information on a newspaper article
    _____ Name
    _____ Author
    _____ Periodical Name
    _____ Volume
    _____ Date
    _____ Page(s)
    _____ Photocopy of part of article
_____ Information on a magazine article
    _____ Name
    _____ Author
    _____ Periodical Name
    _____ Volume
    _____ Date
    _____ Page(s)
    _____ Photocopy of part of article
_____ The call number for a book on the topic
_____ Name of audio/visual resources (if any)

Activity 4: Keep an oral journal

Directions

A. Create a role-play

1. Your teacher will assign you and a partner one of the following role-play situations.
2. Create a role-play. Include expressions from the Overviews on pages x-ref.
3. Use the vocabulary words listed with your role-play. If you aren't sure about the meaning of the vocabulary words, ask your teacher.

Role-play #1

You want to find out if the library has any videos about pollution.

You'd like to take the video home to watch it, if possible.

Vocabulary words:

> on reserve
>
> card catalog
>
> to look up
>
> to check out

Role-play #2

You are going on a trip to Yellowstone National Park next month. You want to see if the library has any travel guides about the park.

Vocabulary words:

> reference area
>
> check out overnight
>
> alphabetical order
>
> reference librarian

Role-play #3

Your professor said he put some old tests "on reserve" at the library. You want to find them and look at them.

Vocabulary words:

    reserve room

    on reserve

    2-hour limit

Role-play #4

You'd like to check out a book, but you don't have a library card yet.

Vocabulary words:

    loan desk

    photo ID

    loan period

    overdue

    fine

B. Record your dialogue

With your partner, record your dialogue on audiocassette for your teacher. As you prepare, look at the following checklist.

_____ We included expressions from the Overviews.

_____ Our sentences show that we understand the vocabulary words.

_____ We practiced our pronunciation and intonation.

C. Perform for your classmates

Your teacher may ask you to perform your dialogue as a role-play in front of the class. Write the vocabulary words you will use on the blackboard before you begin your role-play.

Activity 5: Evaluate your work

Directions

Answer the following questions.

1. What new skill(s) did you learn in this chapter?

2. What skills do you still need to practice?

3. Would you ask a librarian for help if you needed it? Why or why not?

4. If a teacher assigned a research project at the library, would you feel confident about using the library? Why or why not?

CHAPTER TEN

ARGUING YOUR POINT

In this chapter, you will learn how to:
- write a proposition for a debate
- organize your arguments
- prepare your strategy
- present a strong opinion
- disagree politely
- state facts
- use persuasive language
- conclude a debate

RHYTHM PRACTICE

In this chant, you will be introduced to some of the vocabulary and expressions you will use to plan and do a debate.

Directions

1. Listen to the chant.
2. Repeat after your teacher.
3. Practice the chant several times with a partner. One of you reads A, and the other reads B. Read the chorus together.

CHORUS: IS it O.K.?
IS it all RIGHT?
WHAT are the FACTS?
WHAT are their RIGHTS?

A: GUNS over the COUNTer
RIOTS in the STREETS
SMOKING on our CAMpus
The POOR and the eLITE.

(CHORUS)

B: 80 percent say THIS
20 percent say THAT
TRY to prove your POINT
HAVE you got the FACTS?

(CHORUS)

A: GOT to look at BOTH sides
LIST up PROS and CONS
AnTICipate their QUESTions
Be READy to reSPOND.

(CHORUS)

B: REsearch in the STACKS
QUESTions on the STRFFT
HAVE to plan it OUT
WHEN can you guys MEET?

INTRODUCTION TO DEBATE

A debate is a formal argument. Participants choose a **controversial** topic, which is an issue that many people are arguing about. Then a statement, called a **proposition,** is created. Two teams form; one team agrees with what the proposition says, the other team disagrees. The team which agrees is called the "**pro**" side; the team which disagrees is called the "**con**" side. Each team researches the issue, gathers facts, organizes arguments, and prepares a strategy. Each team member gives short speeches, listens carefully to the other team, and asks and answers questions. Debaters always try to use strong, polite language. Debaters hope to convince the audience to agree with their opinion.

The debate is organized in a way to give each side a chance to **persuade** the audience that its argument is **logical** and **supported by facts**, and to **refute** (ask questions, prove wrong) the argument of the other team by showing it is **illogical** or **unsupported by enough facts**. At the end of the debate, each team member **gives a rebuttal** (fixes and repeats his or her argument) as a summary.

To get ready for a debate, you will need to prepare in three ways. First you will need to choose a topic and write a proposition. Then, you will research the topic you have chosen. While you are gathering facts and arguments, you will also need to practice the techniques of making a strong, polite, well-reasoned argument. Then you will be ready to give your debate in front of the class.

MODEL CONVERSATION 1

Directions

1. Read the conversation silently
2. Listen to the model conversation.
3. Divide into pairs or groups of four and divide up the four roles.
4. Read it out loud twice with classmates, changing parts each time.
5. Answer the questions that follow.

(Students have looked through newspapers and interviewed people to find interesting topics to debate. In class, partners discuss topics to suggest to the class.)

Sami: What kinds of issues did you hear about when you interviewed people?

Veronique: Lots of different ones. One that several people mentioned was the problem of homeless people.

Sami: Same here. I know I was surprised to see so many street people when I was travelling. How about choosing homelessness as a debate topic?

Veronique: Yeah, I think it would be interesting. What specifically could we debate about?

Sami: Hmmm. The person I interviewed said people disagree about who is homeless, why they're homeless, and especially on what should be done.

Veronique: We could debate all those things. Maybe we should focus on what should be done.

Sami: Let's suggest that.

(Each pair suggests a topic to the class. Classmates choose topics that interest them and form groups. The teacher asks each group to write a "proposition" and organize research tasks.)

Sami: So does everybody understand what we are supposed to do?

Toshi: Well, we're supposed to make our topic into a statement, right?

Veronique: Yeah, a "proposition" that we can agree or disagree with. Any suggestions?

Wu-Mei: We could say, "Homeless people need to be given a place to sleep"?

Sami: Yeah, and maybe we could make it more specific. How about saying, "This city's government should provide more shelters for the homeless."

Wu-Mei:	I like that. It's specific enough, and someone said that the city only provides a few shelters now.
Veronique:	I don't know much about homelessness, do you guys?
Toshi:	Not really. What's the best way to learn about it?
Sami:	We could do interviews to get the opinions of the students on campus.
Veronique:	Yeah. Or go to the library. Who wants to get information at the library?
Toshi:	I could try, but I might need some help.
Wu-Mei:	I could help with that.
Sami:	I'll come up with some questions and interview some students on campus.
Veronique:	I'll help you. Why don't I interview the teachers in our program?
Wu-Mei:	Let's get together the day after tomorrow and talk about what we've come up with. Does that sound O.K.? Then we can break into teams for the debate.
Sami:	Sounds good.
Toshi:	Wu-Mei, do you want to go to the library right after class?
Wu-Mei:	Yeah. Sure.

Questions on the Model Conversation:

1. How did Veronique and Sami find out about possible debate topics?
2. What phrase did Sami use to suggest a topic?
3. How did Veronique suggest making the topic more specific, or focused?
4. What is a proposition? What proposition did the group working on "homelessness" create?
5. What phrase did Sami use when he wanted to improve on Wu-Mei's proposition?
6. How do the students plan to learn more about homelessness?
7. What phrase did they use to ask for a volunteer?
8. What phrases did they use to volunteer for a research job?
9. When will they meet together? What phrases did Wu-Mei use to organize that meeting time?
10. Do you think they worked well as a group? Why?

SECTION 1: CHOOSING A TOPIC, WRITING A PROPOSITION, AND DIVIDING THE WORKLOAD

Preview Questions

1. What is an argument?

   What is a debate?

   How is it different from a speech?

   How is it different from a discussion?

2. Have you ever participated in or seen a debate?

3. When you work on a group project, how can you organize your research so that everyone shares equally in the work?

Overview 1

Directions

1. Repeat the phrases after your teacher, making notes about intonation and stress.
2. Find some of these expressions in the Model Conversation on pages 216 and 217 and underline them.
3. Try to think of more expressions to add to the Overview.

Choosing a topic and writing a proposition

1. We could talk about (equality between men and women).
   We could say (a woman's role is to raise children).

2. Why don't we debate about (the new non-smoking rule on campus)? How about saying (students should be allowed to smoke in their dorm rooms)?

3. How about talking about (gun control)? Maybe, more specifically, (it should be illegal to own handguns in America).

4. _____

Dividing the workload

1. Who wants to (get information at the library)?

2. Do you want to (interview people) or (work in the library)?

3. So, who is going to (do what)?

4. I could help with (that).

5. Why don't I (make up a questionnaire)?

6. When should we get together next?

7. _____

8. _____

Practice 1.1: Get ideas for debate topics

Directions

A. Interviewing for ideas

Interview other students and people outside of your program about ideas for debate topics. Use the following questions as you gather information.

1. What are some controversial issues in your country? Could you explain each side of the argument?

2. What other problems is your country experiencing? Do people agree on the solutions? Could you explain?

3. What are some problems or conflicts in the world right now? When people talk about these, what do they disagree about?

4. What are some issues or problems around campus, or in student life? Does everyone agree on what should be done?

5. Conflicts often come up in families or other social groups. What are some of the social issues people are facing? Do people agree on the solutions? What do they disagree about?

6. Have you ever watched, or taken part in, a debate? What was the topic? What were the main points of the arguments?

B. Looking for ideas in newspapers

Look through a national, local, and campus newspaper to discover issues in which people disagree with laws or disagree over people's rights. Make a list to share with the class.

C. Brainstorming topics for debate

> When you **brainstorm**, try to come up with many ideas quickly. Say whatever comes into your mind. Don't worry about how good your ideas are. Feel free and let yourself be creative.

1. As a class, or in small groups, brainstorm topics to debate.
2. When your teacher asks for ideas, call out one idea.
3. You, or your teacher, will add the idea to the list on the board.
4. Copy down on a piece of paper the list your class creates.

Practice 1.2: Write a proposition

> A **proposition** is a statement that people can agree or disagree with to make a debate. You need to think about the following points in order to write an effective proposition:
>
> 1. Write a proposition as a statement, not as a question.
>
> 2. Be as specific as possible about who, what, and when.
>
> 3. Make the statement talk about how beliefs or policies should change.
>
> ### Example
> Proposition: Country Y should give foreign aid only when Country X stops violating human rights.
>
> Proposition: Terminally ill patients should be helped to die early if that is what the patients want.
>
> Proposition: More trees should be cut down to enlarge parking lots around campus.

Directions

A. 1. Read each of the propositions on the list below.
   2. Try to improve the form of the proposition by referring to the list in the box on page 220.
   3. Write the improved propositions on the lines provided.

1. Should our country have mandatory military service for men?

   _____

   _____

2. Women shouldn't work.

   _____

   _____

3. Are entrance examinations for college necessary?

   _____

   _____

4. The president should continue his current economic policy.

   _____

   _____

5. Arranged marriages are best.

   _____

   _____

B. 1. With a partner, look at the list of ideas for debate topics which your class made in Practice 1.1 on page 219 and 220. Write propositions for those that interest you the most.
   2. Your teacher will ask each of you to write some propositions on the blackboard.
   3. The class will choose one proposition to prepare for the final class debate, or students may form groups by topic of interest.

Practice 1.3: Do background research and interviews

Directions

A. Divide the workload

1. The teacher will divide the class into groups. Within each group, members should form two teams. One team will prepare for the "pro" argument. The other team will prepare for the "con" side of the final debate.

2. Use the expressions from the Overview on page 219 to discuss how you will divide the research workload. Discuss:

_____ researching at the library

_____ summarizing the research

_____ preparing an interview

_____ interviewing knowledgeable people

_____ when and where to meet and discuss your findings

B. Do research at the library

1. Find three articles on your topic.
2. Read them; make photocopies if you'd like.
3. Summarize or take notes on note-cards.
4. Share the summaries and notes with team members.
5. Keep your notes for use in later exercises and in the final debate.
6. Turn in a summary or note-card for each of your three sources for your teacher to check. Use the summary form on page 322, Appendix 2. Look at the following example of a notecard.

Time: DECEMBER 17, 1990. "Answers at Last," p 44–49.

In a stunning social blunder, patients were released from public institutions and given no place to go—no halfway house, no local clinics, no community care. Between 1960 and 1984, the population in mental institutions fell from 544, 000 to 134,000.

C. Interview knowledgeable people

1. Prepare questions.
2. Interview as many people as you can who know about the topic.
3. Take notes or record your interview.
4. Share what you learned with the other members of your group.
5. Turn in an interview form with notes. Use the form on page 323, Appendix 2.

MODEL CONVERSATION 2

● ●

Directions

1. Read the conversation silently.
2. Listen to the model conversation.
3. Read it out loud twice with a classmate, changing roles each time.
4. Answer the questions that follow.

(Ricardo and Jeff are preparing to talk to their landlord about a problem.)

Jeff: You know, Ricardo, we should talk to Mr. Elliot about the deposit on our apartment. We did a really good job cleaning up when we moved out, but he only gave us back half of our damage deposit. That's $150 we lost.

Ricardo: Yeah. I know. But we need to think about what we're going to say.

Jeff: O.K. Well, I'll call him up and ask if we can talk about why he kept some of our deposit.

Ricardo: What can we say if he says "I had to have the screens on two windows replaced" ?

Jeff: If he says that, then we should say "They were broken when we moved in."

Ricardo: Yeah, but, what facts do we have?

Jeff: Well, we have that checklist we did on the apartment before we signed the lease. That says the screens were already broken.

Ricardo: Sounds good.

(Jeff calls up Mr. Elliot)

Mr. Elliot: Hello?

Jeff: Hi Mr. Elliot, this is Jeff Nelson. Ricardo and I rented an apartment from you . . .

Mr. Elliot: Oh hello, Jeff, I remember. You two just moved out of 213. How can I help you?

Jeff: Could we talk about the damage deposit?

Mr. Elliot: Yeah. Of course.

Jeff: Ricardo and I thought we left the place in good shape, so weren't we supposed to get another $150 back?

Mr. Elliot: I'm afraid I have to disagree, Jeff. I had to have the rugs steam-cleaned and those two window screens replaced.

Jeff: I understand some work was needed, but that doesn't mean that we were responsible. The move-in checklist we did when we signed our lease shows that the screens were already broken.

Mr. Elliot: Well, if the checklist shows that they were already broken, of course I can return some of your deposit. I'm sure that you agree the carpets needed cleaning, though, don't you?

Jeff: I understand about the carpets. I thought they were O.K., but they probably needed steam cleaning. We were mostly concerned about paying for the broken screens.

Mr. Elliot: Sounds like there was a mix-up with the property management people. I'll talk to them and they, or I, will get back to you tomorrow. Does that sound O.K.?

Jeff: Great. And thank you. Talk to you then.

Questions on the Model Conversation:

1. What problem do Jeff and Ricardo have? Why do they want to talk to Mr. Elliot?

2. Do you think it was helpful to plan their conversation first? Why?

3. What phrases did they use as they planned what they would say?

4. What made Jeff and Ricardo's argument strong?

5. What phrases did Jeff and Mr. Elliot use when they disagreed?

6. Jeff and Mr. Elliot agree that the screens need fixing. They disagree on the cause. How does Jeff express his disagreement?

Section 2: Preparing the Argument

Preview Questions

1. What are debates used for in your culture? Is public policy decided this way?

2. If people disagree in public, do they continue to argue or does everyone change the subject? How do you feel when you have to disagree with someone?

3. Have you ever had to speak in English when you needed to convince someone that they were wrong and you were right?

Overview 2

Directions

1. Repeat the phrases after your teacher, making notes about intonation and stress.
2. Find some of these expressions in the Model Conversation on pages 223 and 224 and underline them.
3. Try to think of more expressions to add to the Overview.

Planning your arguments

1. What do you think about (the new non-smoking rule)? What are the pros and cons?

2. What facts do we have? What examples can we give?

3. Are there any holes in our argument?

4. What will the other side say?

5. _____

6. _____

Preparing your strategy

1. What can we say if they say ("smoking causes cancer")?

2. If they say, ("it's natural for women to raise kids"), then we should say ("in some cultures men or women do").

3. What questions will we ask them? What questions do you think they will ask?

4. What points should each person make?

5. _____

6. _____

Practice 2.1 Prepare for an argument

Directions

A. Read the situation below. Later in the chapter you will role-play this situation.

SITUATION: Returning something to the store

STORE MANAGER: Yesterday was the last day of a holiday sale in which everything was sold for half-price. You are glad that so much of the old merchandise is gone, because you need room for new stock. Usually, you accept returned merchandise because you want your customers to be happy. During your big sales, however, you always post a sign which says "No returns on sale items."

CUSTOMER: You often shop at this store, and have returned things in the past without any problem. Yesterday you saw a hair-dryer there for a very good price, and bought it. When you got home, the hair-dryer worked, but you decided you didn't like the way it dried your hair. You want to return it and get your money back.

B. Discuss the following questions with a classmate.

1. Should the store manager return the customer's money? Why or why not?

2. What is the opposite point of view on that?

3. What facts could the store manager use to support his or her point of view?

4. What facts could the customer use to support his or her point of view?

5. What arguments could the customer use to convince the store manager?

6. How could the store manager convince the customer that he or she needs to follow a "no returns" policy?

C. 1. Your teacher will assign you the role of "customer" or "manager."
    2. Find other classmates with the same role to plan for an argument between the "customer" and the "manager." Make groups of three or four.
    3. Use the expressions for "Preparing your strategy" on page 225 to discuss how your character can best present his or her side of the argument.
    4. Prepare a list of arguments on the following chart that you can use when you role-play this situation later in the chapter.

What you could say	What the other character might say

SECTION 3: ARGUING POLITELY

Preview Questions

1. It's easy to say "You're wrong!," but how can you say that more politely?

2. Is it possible to agree with part of what someone said, but not agree with another part? How could you respond in that situation?

3. What does "to persuade" mean? What language can you use to persuade someone to agree with you?

Overview 3

Directions

1. Repeat the phrases after your teacher, making notes about intonation and stress.
2. Find some of these expressions in the Model Conversation on pages 223 and 224 and underline them.
3. Try to think of more expressions to add to the Overview.

Presenting a strong opinion

1. Of course, (endangered animals must be protected).

2. We really think that (it is natural for women to take care of children).

3. We're convinced that (racism is a problem).

4. We strongly believe that (smoking should be allowed in dorm rooms).

5. _____

6. _____

Disagreeing politely

1. I'm afraid I disagree with you, (Samuel). (People's lives are more important than animal's lives.)

2. I understand what you're saying, but (children need their mothers more than their fathers).

3. I can see your point, but I think you're overlooking something.

4. I can understand your concerns about (that), but . . .

5. _____

6. _____

Persuading

1. Isn't (nature important to our lives)?

2. Wouldn't you agree that (men can take care of children)?

3. Don't you think that (people have the right to choose)?

4. I'm sure that you would agree that (alcohol causes more problems than smoking).

5. You agree (that it is a problem), don't you?

6. _____

7. _____

Practice 3.1: Present a strong argument and disagree politely

Directions

1. Reread the situation involving a customer and a manager in practice 2.1 on page 226.
2. Look at the notes you prepared in part C of that exercise.
3. Find a partner who prepared the opposite role. Make a customer/manager pair.
4. Role-play the discussion they might have. Use expressions from the Overview on pages 228 and 229 to present a strong argument and disagree politely.
5. When your teacher says to change partners, role-play the argument again. Your teacher may ask you to perform your role-play for the class.

Practice 3.2: Use persuasive language

> Choosing to start, or end, a question with a negative expression has a special meaning. It means you EXPECT the person to agree with what you say. This makes it a little more difficult for a person to say "No" to your idea. These kinds of sentences are examples of "persuasive" language.

> ## Example
>
> (You want to persuade me that the teachers in this program are great.)
>
> "AREN'T the TEACHERS in this program GREAT?" (or)
> "You think the TEACHERS in this program are GREAT, don't you?"
>
> (Which means: "I really expect you to agree with me that the teachers in this program are great.")

Directions

A. With a partner, take turns using various expressions from the Overview on page 229 to make these phrases more persuasive.

1. We need less homework.
2. Our parents expect us to study.
3. Students should be paid to study.
4. Learning is a great opportunity.
5. We spend too many years in school.
6. We need more education in our modern world.

B. With a partner, take turns making the following statements into more persuasive questions. Refer to Overview 3 on page 229 to practice different ways of doing this.

1. Homeless shelters are more expensive in the long run.
2. If people are homeless it is their own fault.
3. Homeless people want to work and have a home.
4. Having homeless people on the street is a shame in a rich country.
5. People need a place to live before they can really look for work.
6. Without enough shelters people will sleep on the streets.
7. Many of the homeless are drug or alcohol abusers.
8. Homeless people need job training.

Practice 3.3 Argue strongly and persuasively with a partner

Directions

Use various expressions from the Overview on pages 228 and 229. Take
turns arguing as Partner A and Partner B.

1. **Partner A:** (Express the statement in column "A" as a strong opinion.)

2. **Partner B:** (Respond by making the statement in column B into a more
persuasive statement.)

Example

A	B
1. Women are biologically suited to taking care of children	1. Men can take care of children well.

A: Of course, women are biologically suited to taking care of children.

B: But, wouldn't you agree that men can take care of children well?

A	B
1. Nature is important to our lives and the future .	1. Jobs are more important to our lives now.
2. Smoking should not be allowed because it causes cancer.	2. Alcohol causes more problems than smoking.
3. Rain forests need to be protected.	3. Countries need to use their natural resources to develop.
4. America has many problems with racism.	4. Racism exists in every country.
5. Men need higher salaries than women because they must support their families.	5. In many families, the mother is the only one working.
6. The easy purchase of handguns increases gun-related crimes.	6. People need guns to protect themselves from criminals.
7. The death penalty is needed to punish serious crimes.	7. The death penalty teaches that killing is O.K.
8. Sixteen-year-olds are too irresponsible to drive.	8. Many sixteen-year-olds need their own transportation.

MODEL CONVERSATION 3: A FORMAL DEBATE

Directions

1. Read the conversation silently.
2. Listen to the model conversation.
3. Read it out loud in groups of five.
4. Read it out loud again, changing roles.
5. Answer the questions that follow.

(Veronique and Toshi are debating against Wu-Mei and Sami. The room is arranged for a debate, and vocabulary words have been written on the board and explained.)

Moderator: Today we will debate the following **proposition** "The city should provide more shelters for the homeless." Let's begin with **Pro argument #1**.

Veronique: What should be done for the homeless? Our team strongly believes that we need to build more shelters. *The City Herald* stated last month that the two shelters we have in this town are overcrowded. The people in charge of the local shelter estimate that over 50 percent of the homeless sleep on the streets. The city should spend money now on buying or building the shelters that are needed.

Moderator: Let's hear **Con argument #1** now.

Wu-Mei: Temporary shelters are short-term solutions. The homeless are still homeless. The city shouldn't waste its money on "bandaids." There could be a better solution. The most important thing is to build houses and provide job training for the homeless.

Moderator: **Pro argument #2**, please.

Toshi: I can understand what you're saying, Wu-Mei. Building new homes does sound perfect, however, it is not realistic. It is expensive and the city doesn't have enough money to do that. And this article in *Time* magazine shows that many of these people have real problems. They are alcoholics, drug addicts, and mental patients. So, this shows that they can't take care of homes. They can't even take care of themselves.

Moderator: **Con argument #2**, now.

Sami: I'm afraid I disagree with Toshi. Just because some of the homeless people are alcoholics or mental patients doesn't mean they all are, or even that most of them are. Although that example may be true, it's not generally the case. More and more of the homeless people are families. According to *The New York Times*, in many places 50 percent of the homeless coming to shelters are single mothers with children. Shelters are no solution for them. How can you look for a job and raise children when you have nowhere to live, just a shelter to rest in at night? You even need an address to qualify for government assistance! And . . .

Moderator: I'm sorry, Sami, but your time is up. We now have **question time**. Would the Con side like to start?

Wu-Mei: Veronique, I understand what you're saying, but wouldn't you agree that shelters are just a temporary solution?

Veronique: Shelters are an important, immediate solution. You can't worry about long-range solutions until people have a place to sleep.

Toshi: Wu-Mei, your point about "bandaids" wasn't clear. Could you go over that again?

Wu-Mei: Temporary shelters are a short-term solution. They don't cure the illness, they just cover it up, like a bandaid. The homeless are still homeless.

Moderator: Does the Pro side have any questions?

Toshi: Wu-Mei, how much money would it cost to build housing or give training to every homeless person?

Wu-Mei: Well, I don't mean we should build individual housing for each homeless person; of course that would be too expensive. But we need to think about long-term solutions.

Moderator: Does either side have more questions?

Sami: Toshi, do you believe all homeless people are like the alcoholics or strange people we see on the streets?

Toshi: I strongly believe that many do have serious problems. The February 4th edition of *Time* magazine states that "When many of the mental institutions had to close because of lack of money, patients ended up on the streets."

Veronique: Sami, wouldn't you agree that without enough shelters these people will sleep on the street tonight?

Sami: Of course they need a place to sleep, but the city will spend all of its money on symptoms and nothing on helping people change their lives. Rehabilitation centers would help end the need for shelters.

Moderator: It's time for Rebuttals now. Is the **Pro rebuttal** ready?

Veronique: To conclude, the homeless people need a roof over their head now. Think about tonight. Not later. It may be a short-term solution, but the people out there on the streets are thinking about tonight. Decide that we should build more shelters. Thank you.

Moderator: Con rebuttal #1?

Wu-Mei: To sum up, we need to use our money to start a real change. Remember that shelters are a waste of money because the homeless still have no homes and no hope. Realize that we need houses and help, not temporary shelters. We can't help everyone, but we can make a true start. Think about giving homeless families a new start by building homes and rehabilitation centers. Thank you.

Moderator: Pro rebuttal #2?

Toshi: The city only has a limited amount of money. We can't make most people live on the streets while we find the perfect solution for a few others. Many of the homeless will never be able to work or take care of their own home. Shelters are a solution for everyone. Remember that other projects, like homes and rehabilitation centers, don't help enough people and are expensive.

Moderator: Con rebuttal #2?

Sami: We need to change our image of the homeless, and the image they have about themselves. Many homeless people can be helped. Remember that retraining and a place of their own will take away their need for shelter not only for tonight, but for every other night, too. It's a long-term solution that is a good investment. Decide against the temporary solution of more shelters.

Moderator: Thank you all for a fine debate.

Questions about the Model Conversation:

1. Who belongs to the team "for" building shelters?
2. Who belongs to the team "against" building shelters?
3. Look at the outline of the debate and answer the questions which follow.

Statement of the proposition

Pro argument #1	(2–3 minutes)
Con argument #1	(2–3 minutes)
Pro argument #2	(2–3 minutes)
Con argument #2	(2–3 minutes)
Question period	(8 minutes)
Pro #1 rebuttal	(2 minutes)
Con #1 rebuttal	(2 minutes)
Pro #2 rebuttal	(2 minutes)
Con #2 rebuttal	(2 minutes)

---

    a. Who introduced the proposition?
    b. Who gave the first Pro argument? The second?
    c. Who asked questions during the question time?
    d. Who gave a rebuttal?
    e. How were the rebuttals different from the arguments?
    f. Which team spoke first? last?

4. What was the role of the moderator?
5. Sami questions the reasoning behind Toshi's statement that most homeless people are alcoholics or mentally ill. What language does he use to do this?

Section 4: Interpreting Facts and Examples

Preview Questions

1. What is the difference between an opinion and a fact?

2. Where can you find facts?

3. If you don't understand the point someone is trying to make, what can you do?

Overview 4

Directions

1. Repeat the phrases after your teacher, making notes about intonation and stress.
2. Find some of these expressions in the Model Conversation on pages 232, 233, and 234 and underline them.
3. Try to think of more expressions to add to the Overview.

Stating facts

1. According to (the October 24th edition of *The New York Times*), (most women work because they have to).

2. It says in (*Time* Magazine, July 2nd, 1994) that (handguns are the main cause of violent death in America).

3. The most important fact is that (80 percent of the students we interviewed want smoking on campus).

4. (One study/researcher/article) says that (smoking causes cancer in the children of people who smoke).

5. _____

6. _____

Interpreting facts or examples

1. This fact shows (that women can't stay home with their children).

2. This means that (fewer handguns would mean fewer deaths).

3. So, in other words (students believe smoking isn't a problem).

4. Therefore, (innocent people are harmed by other people's smoking).

5. _____

6. _____

Practice 4.1: State facts and clarify meaning

Directions

In this exercise, you and a partner will use Overview 4 on pages 236 and 237 phrases to practice stating facts, asking for clarification, and interpreting facts.

1. Each of you will look at a different box. Look at the notes in your box.
2. Tell your partner the quote, and state the source. Try to use a variety of expressions from the Overview.
3. When your partner asks for clarification, use the interpretation listed to explain the meaning.
4. When it is your partner's turn to explain, listen carefully and write down the missing information in your chart.

Example

You: According to *The New York Times*, "There has been a 30 percent increase in homicides since Mayor Jason took office."

Your partner: Your last point wasn't clear, could you go over it again?

You: Murders have increased by 30 percent. This means that Mayor Jason's new policy is a disaster.

Student A look here:

SOURCE	QUOTE	INTERPRETATION
1. *The New York Times*	The president's popularity rating went down 10 percent after his European visit.	People were unhappy with the president's foreign policy.
2.	63 percent of the high school students who were tested couldn't identify Japan on a map of the world.	
3. *Time Magazine*	Seattle consumes more espresso and other coffee products than any other city in North America.	Espresso is extremely popular in Seattle.
4.	Tuition will be raised to keep pace with the ever-increasing costs of running the university.	
5. The National Institute of Health	Extensive trials show that the new influenza medicine diminishes associated symptoms.	People who use this drug when they have the flu feel better.
6.	Stress is directly associated with increased insomnia.	

Student B look here:

SOURCE	QUOTE	INTERPRETATION
1.	The president's popularity rating went down 10 percent after his European visit.	
2. The State Board of Education	63 percent of the high school students who were tested couldn't identify Japan on a map of the world.	Most high school students know very little about the world or geography.
3.	Seattle consumes more espresso and other coffee products than any other city in North America.	
4. The President of this college	Tuition will be raised to keep pace with the ever-increasing costs of running the university.	You can expect tuition to go up if costs go up.
5.	Extensive trials show that the new influenza medicine diminishes associated symptoms.	
6. Dr. Jack Nelson	Stress is directly associated with increased insomnia.	People who have trouble sleeping should try to lower their stress level.

Practice 4.2: State facts from your research

In practice 1.3 on page 222, your group did research and interviewed knowledgeable people about the proposition for the final class debate. What facts and information has your group found?

Directions

1. Write down the most important facts and where you found them.
2. Practice stating and explaining each one with a partner from your group.

SOURCE/ DATE	QUOTE	INTERPRETATION
1.		
2.		
3.		
4.		
5.		
6.		

SECTION 5: REFUTING AND SUMMING UP

Preview Questions

1. Can people agree on the facts but disagree on what the facts mean?
2. What is reasoning? Can you think of an example of poor reasoning?
3. What is a generalization? What is a problem with using generalizations?
4. At the end of a speech or a debate, what do you want the audience to remember?

Overview 5

Directions

1. Repeat the phrases after your teacher, making notes about intonation and stress.
2. Find some of these expressions in the Model Conversation on pages 232, 233, and 234 and underline them.
3. Try to think of more expressions to add to the Overview.

Refuting

1. Just because (men haven't traditionally looked after children) doesn't mean (men can't).
2. Although that example may be true, it's not generally the case. By contrast . . .
3. It's not the same situation. You can't compare things that are so different.
4. There could be another explanation for that. For example . . .
5. I'm not sure (about your facts.)

Rebutting/Summing up

1. To conclude, (logging companies should stop cutting down the rain forests).
2. To sum up, (men and women are both able to take care of children).

Convincing

1. Remember that (we must save the forest's important plants and animals).
2. Decide that (saving nature is more important than making money).
3. Recognize that (each family should be able to decide who will stay home and who will go to work).

Practice 5.1: Refute the reasoning

One of the most important skills in debates is the ability to recognize mistakes in the reasoning of your opponents. Here are several important questions to ask yourself as you listen to statements and prepare questions. Notice how expressions from the Overview on page 241 are used to refute the reasoning.

a. What are the sources? Are they recent? Are they reliable or knowledgeable?

Poor evidence: "According to my roommate, murderers deserve the death penalty.

Refuting: "I'm not sure about your sources. According to experts on the justice system . . . "

b. Are there enough examples? Are there enough facts?

Lack of evidence: "Based on a survey (of three), all Americans agree that nuclear power is dangerous."

Refuting: "I'm not sure you have all the facts. For instance, a survey of 3,000 Americans reported in Time magazine says . . . "

c. Is the statement true in all cases? Are the examples typical?

Generalization: "All homeless people are alcoholics. You can see them on the streets downtown."

Refuting: "Although the homeless you see downtown may be alcoholics, it's not generally the case. You just don't see all the homeless mothers and kids."

d. Could there be another cause? Could there be another explanation?

Unclear cause: "The number of homeless people using shelters dropped by 25% in the last three months, so the government's policy is working."

Refuting: "There could be another explanation for that. For example, it has been summertime."

e. Are the subjects being compared the same? Are there important differences?

Poor comparison: "Gun control has worked well in Japan and so it would work well in the United States.

Refuting: "It's not the same situation. You can't compare cultures that are so different."

Directions

1. Discuss with a partner what is wrong with each of the statements below.
2. Take turns reading a statement out loud and having your partner challenge the reasoning. Use various expressions from page 241 to refute the arguments.

STATEMENTS

1. He did poorly in his schoolwork, so he will do poorly as a professional businessman.

2. I know you can catch AIDS from sharing food because my roommate told me so.

3. Americans believe the president should not be re-elected. I interviewed six people and 100 percent of them said the president was doing a bad job.

4. Jimmy Carter and Bill Clinton are both from the South, so they have very similar politics.

5. Female animals naturally take care of the young while the male provides food and protection; women were meant to stay home.

6. Cigarettes, marijuana, cocaine, and alcohol are all common drugs, so the laws should be the same for them all.

7. Jake always gets higher marks on his tests than John. Jake must be more intelligent.

8. It only took me six months to become fluent in French, so it should only take you six months to become fluent in English.

9. A pair of stolen shoes was found in her room. She must have stolen them.

10. Dogs have needed to be leashed for years, so cats should be, too.

11. Germany reunited successfully, so Korea can, too.

12. Horatio Alger came to America as a poor immigrant and became rich. Therefore the American Dream is true.

13. The TOEFL scores of the students in this program have improved, so we know our TOEFL prep class is effective.

14. My roommates live on pizza. American eating habits are terrible.

15. The high percentage of blacks in professional sports is proof of their physical superiority.

Practice 5.2: Check your own logic

Directions

Look at the list of facts and interpretations which you prepared in Practice 4.2 on page 240. With a partner from your debate group, discuss the following questions:

1. How is the quality of our sources? Any poor evidence?

2. How about the quantity of our evidence? Any lack of evidence?

3. How is our reasoning?

    a. Are there any poor generalizations?

    b. Are the causes clear?

    c. Are there any poor comparisons? Could the same facts be explained differently?

Practice 5.3: Sum up and make a rebuttal

> "Summing up" is your last chance to convince the audience that your team's opinion is the correct opinion. You want the audience to remember your most important points.

Directions

1. Partner A: Begin by summing up the "PRO" argument on the next page. Use expressions from the Overview on page 241.
2. Partner B: Look at page 246 and take notes on the main idea and reasons given.
3. Switch roles. Partner B should now explain the "CON" argument, while Partner A takes notes.

Student A look here:

PRO ARGUMENT

Proposition: There should be no smoking in the dormitories.

Main idea: Smoking is dangerous and should not be allowed in dorm rooms.

Reasons:
1. The local fire department believes smoking in the dorms is very dangerous.
2. Smoking is bad for the students' health, so they need to break the habit sometime.
3. Living in the dorms could be less expensive with cheaper, non-smoking insurance.

CON ARGUMENT

Proposition: There should be no smoking in the dormitories.

Main idea:

Reasons:
1.

2.

3.

Student B look here:

PRO ARGUMENT
Proposition: There should be no smoking in the dormitories.
Main idea:
Reasons: 1.
2.
3.

CON ARGUMENT
Proposition: There should be no smoking in the dormitories
Main idea: Smoking is an individual freedom that should be allowed in dorm rooms.
Reasons: 1.   95 percent of the students we talked to believe smoking is a personal choice.
2.   Smoking lets students relax and feel at home.
3.   Twenty accidents happened in the dorms because of alcohol. None happened because of smoking.

Activity 1: Role-play polite arguments

Directions

Use all the Overview expressions you have studied to prepare one of the
role-plays below. Sit with a partner, or in a small group, and choose one of
the roles for each situation below.

1. Organize the arguments.
2. Prepare a strategy.
3. Practice expressing strong, polite opinions.
4. When everyone is ready, find a partner who has practiced the other role,
   and role-play together.
5. You may present it for the class, or practice again with another partner.

SITUATIONS

A. Questioning your grade in a class

TEACHER: The quarter is finished and you've given grades out to your students.
You only give "As" to students who are really outstanding. You were tired when
you did the grades; you might have made a few mistakes. A student comes to
ask you about his or her grade. You remember that this student didn't talk very
much in class discussions.

STUDENT: You kept track of your grades on all your tests and quizzes, so you
were surprised when your friend got an A and you only got a B-. You two had
almost the same test scores. You are shy in discussions, but you were always
there and prepared.

B. Getting a job on campus

TUTOR COORDINATOR: You like to hire tutors that are very good math and
English students and who can explain things well. You believe that being
sensitive to students who are having problems is important, too. In the past,
you have always hired native speakers to do tutoring, and you worry that a
non-native speaker might be too difficult to understand.

FOREIGN STUDENT: You'd like to get a job on campus doing tutoring. You
have a light accent, but you never have big problems being understood by
others. You studied math for the last two quarters and received an "A" each
time. You enjoy helping others.

Activity 2: Do impromptu debates

Directions

1. Make groups of four.
2. Break into pro and con pairs.
3. With your partner, spend just 10 minutes organizing your arguments and preparing a strategy.
4. Then begin your debate. Your debate should last about 8 to 10 minutes.
5. Your teacher may ask you to present your debate to the class.

Choose from the following topics, or create a new topic.

Debate the benefits of:

1. winter versus summer

2. meat-eating versus vegetarianism

3. cats versus dogs as pets

4. cars versus bicycles

5. school uniforms versus free dress

6. tests versus no tests

7. studying English in your own country versus studying it overseas

8. being a female versus being a male

9. apartments versus houses

10. having kids versus remaining childless

Activity 3: Prepare for the class debate

Directions

Review the phrases and techniques you have studied in this chapter as you prepare an outline for your final class debate.

1. Make a debate pair with someone who has prepared the same side of the debate.
2. Prepare the outline below.
3. Review practices 1.2 (your proposition), 1.3 (your research), 4.2 (state facts), and 5.2 (check your logic).
4. As you plan your strategy, decide how to express your opinions, and prepare your rebuttal, referring to the Overviews on pages 219, 225, 236, and 237.

OUTLINE FOR THE CLASS DEBATE:

PROPOSITION: _____

_____

First Argument (2 to 3 minutes)
Fact/example
Fact/example
Summary/Clarification

Second Argument (2 to 3 minutes)
Fact/example
Fact/example
Summary/Clarification

Possible Con Questions and Pro Responses (4 minutes)

Possible Pro Questions and Con Responses (4 minutes)

Rebuttal 1 (2 minutes)

Rebuttal 2 (2 minutes)

Activity 4: Keep an oral journal

Directions

Prepare for the class debate by practicing expressing your opinions and arguments.

1. On audiocassette, record what you plan to say during the class debate. Your teacher will listen to the cassette and record suggestions on how you can improve the performance or content of your argument before the in-class debate.

2. Use an audio or video cassette to rehearse your debate. With a partner from your group, or with the entire group, run through a practice debate. You will need to role-play what the opposite team might say. Your teacher may listen to your rehearsal or critique your audio or video recording.

Activity 5: Hold the class debate

A. Performing your debate

Directions

1. Write the proposition on the board.
2. Arrange the class so that the debate teams are on opposite sides. Make room for the audience, if you have one.
3. Write any important, new vocabulary words on the board and explain them to the audience so that they can understand the debate more easily.
4. Choose someone to time the arguments.
5. Your teacher may moderate (direct or control the debate) or ask a student to moderate.

B. Listening to debates

Listen carefully to each debate and take notes. Then fill out the debate summary form in Appendix 2, page 234, and turn it in to your teacher.

Activity 6: Evaluate your work

Directions

1. Use this form to critique your own performance, either as you watch the debate on video, or directly after the debate.
2. Compare your critique with the feedback that your teacher gives you.
3. If the teacher and class agree, and there is time, try debating the same topic again for a better performance or evaluation. Go back and do more research where your data was lacking. Practice more!

YOUR PERFORMANCE

prepared carefully	YES	SOMEWHAT	NO
spoke clearly	YES	SOMEWHAT	NO
spoke with stress and emotion	YES	SOMEWHAT	NO
used polite, strong language	YES	SOMEWHAT	NO

ARGUMENTS

prepared facts	YES	SOMEWHAT	NO
presented clearly	YES	SOMEWHAT	NO
argued logically	YES	SOMEWHAT	NO
refuted actively	YES	SOMEWHAT	NO
answered questions	YES	SOMEWHAT	NO
used persuasive language	YES	SOMEWHAT	NO
rebutted strongly	YES	SOMEWHAT	NO

COMMENTS

CHAPTER ELEVEN

VISITING A COLLEGE CLASS

In this chapter you will practice language to help
you visit a college classroom and improve your
understanding of what regular college courses are
like. You will learn how to:

- get information about a class
- contact a department and instructor
- ask permission to visit a class
- talk about your expectations and worries
- ask for advice and give advice

RHYTHM PRACTICE

In this chant, you will be introduced to some expressions you can use when organizing a visit to a college class.

Directions

1. Listen to the chant.
2. Repeat after your teacher.
3. Practice the chant several times with a partner. One of you reads A, and the other reads B.

A: Could you sugGEST a CLASS?
Could you sugGEST a CLASS?
Could you sugGEST a CLASS to TAKE, CLASS to TAKE?

B: If I were YOU I'd try
If I were YOU I'd try
If I were YOU I'd try THIS one, try THIS one.

A: Could you TELL me if
Could you TELL me if
Could you TELL me if he's IN, if he's IN?

B: Just a SEC and I'LL CHECK
Just a SEC and I'LL CHECK
Just a SEC and I'll CHECK and SEE, CHECK and SEE.

A: May I COME to your CLASS?
May I COME to your CLASS?
May I COME to your CLASS this WEEK, CLASS this WEEK?

B: Of COURSE you can come
Of COURSE you can come
Of COURSE you can come ANYtime, ANYtime.

MODEL CONVERSATION

Directions

1. Read the conversation silently.
2. Listen to the model conversation.
3. Read it out loud twice with a classmate, changing roles each time.
4. Answer the questions that follow.

(Veronique meets Eduardo at the coffee shop on campus.)

Eduardo: Hi Veronique!

Veronique: Hi Eduardo! Long time no see. How've you been?

Eduardo: Good. And I heard that you were accepted into the university for fall quarter!

Veronique: Yeah. It's exciting, but I feel kind of nervous.

Eduardo: What are you worried about?

Veronique: Well, I'm afraid I might not understand the lectures. I guess I don't know what to expect, really. Do you know what I mean?

Eduardo: I know how you feel, but don't worry. If I were you, I'd try to visit some classes and see what they are like.

Veronique: What class would you recommend visiting?

Eduardo: Why don't you visit my Anthropology 102 class?

Veronique: When does it meet?

Eduardo: Monday through Thursday at 10:00.

Veronique: Is it O.K. for me to just show up?

Eduardo: You'd better ask the professor first. His name is Stevenson.

Veronique: I feel nervous about talking to American professors. What's he like?

Eduardo: He's really nice.

Veronique: O.K., I'll give it a try!

(Veronique goes to the Anthropology Department to talk with the secretary.)

Secretary: Can I help you with something?

Veronique: Yes, please. I'd like to talk with Professor Stevenson, is he in?

Secretary: Let me see . . . (*She looks at a schedule form.*). I'm afraid he's in class right now.

Veronique:	Could you tell me when his office hours are?
Secretary:	He has office hours from 1:00 to 3:00 on Wednesdays.
Veronique:	I'll stop by on Wednesday; thanks for your help.
	(Veronique returns on Wednesday at 2:00 and knocks on Professor Stevenson's door.)
Professor Stevenson:	Come on in.
Veronique:	Hello Professor Stevenson. My name is Veronique Dupont.
Professor Stevenson:	Nice to meet you, Veronique. What can I do for you?
Veronique:	I'm from Belgium and I'm at this university studying English in the Intensive English Program. I'd like to visit your Anthropology 102 class one time, if that's O.K. with you?
Professor Stevenson:	Really? How come?
Veronique:	Well, I plan to start classes here soon and want to see what classes are like. I'm very interested in anthropology, and one of my friends told me he really enjoyed your class. Could I sit in on the class once?
Professor Stevenson:	That'd be fine. When were you thinking of coming?
Veronique:	May I come next week sometime?
Professor Stevenson:	Any day except Monday is fine. They have a test then.
Veronique:	Thank you very much! I'm looking forward to visiting your class.
Professor Stevenson:	Good. See you there.

Questions about the Model Conversation:

1. How does Veronique explain about her worries?
2. What phrases does she use to ask Eduardo for advice?
3. What phrases does Eduardo use to give Veronique advice?
4. How does Veronique choose a class to visit?
5. What does Veronique need to do before she visits the class?
6. What information does she need to contact the professor?
7. How does she ask permission to visit the class? What kind of language does she use?
8. What do you think about Eduardo's advice?

SECTION 1: ASKING FOR AND GIVING ADVICE

Preview Questions

1. Have you ever visited a college class taught in English? Why or why not? If you have, tell about your experience.

2. How will it help you to visit a college class before you take it for credit?

3. Do you ever dream or worry about taking classes with American students and professors? What do you imagine?

Overview 1

Directions

1. Repeat the phrases after your teacher, making notes about intonation and stress.
2. Find some of these expressions in the Model Conversation on pages 255 and 256 and underline them.
3. Try to think of more expressions to add to the Overview.

Talking about your worries / asking for advice

1. I feel nervous about (talking to professors). Do you know what I mean?

2. I don't know if I'll be able to (understand the lecture). Do you have any suggestions for me?

3. I'm worried about (keeping up with my American classmates). How can I (prepare for starting regular classes)?

4. I'm afraid I might (fail the essay examinations). Can you suggest (a good way to prepare for them)?

5. _____

6. _____

Giving advice

1. Don't worry. Why don't you (start trying to meet professors now)?

2. It can be difficult, but I'd suggest (using a tape recorder or the note-taking service on campus).

3. If I were you, I would try to (have American students study with you).

4. I'd really recommend (visiting the class this quarter).

5. _____

6. _____

Practice 1.1: Ask for and give advice

Student A look here:

Directions

A. You are a worried student. Use various expressions from the Overview on page 257 to ask your partner for advice about the worries listed on the chart below. Take notes on the advice your partner gives you.

Example

Worried Student: I'm afraid I might not understand the textbooks. Do you know what I mean?

Friend: Sure I do. If I were you, I'd buy my textbooks during the break and start reading them early.

Your Worries	Partner's Advice
1. You are scared to talk to the professor in his office.	_____
2. You don't know what classes to take.	_____
3. You might have difficulty finishing the homework.	_____

B. Now, change roles. You are a friend giving advice. Write down notes about your partner's worries. Use various expression from the Overview to give the advice suggested in the chart below.

Partner's Worries	Your Advice
1. _____	Get suggestions from other international students.
2. _____	Read the syllabus very carefully the first day.
3. _____	Ask an American student in your class if you can copy his or her notes or study together.

Student B look here:

Directions

A. You are the friend of a worried student. Take notes as your partner asks for advice. Use various expressions from the Overview on page 257 to give the advice listed on the chart below.

Example

Worried Student: I'm afraid I might not understand the textbooks. Do you know what I mean?

Friend: Sure I do. If I were you, I'd buy my textbooks during the break and start reading them early.

Partner's Worries	Your Advice
1. _____ _____	Talk to your instructor for a few minutes right after class.
2. _____ _____	Ask American students and international students for suggestions on good classes.
3. _____ _____	Start building good study habits now.

B. Now, change roles. You are a worried student. Use various expressions from the Overview to ask your partner for advice about the worries listed on the chart below. Take notes on the advice your partner gives you.

Your Worries	Partner's Advice
1. You don't know the best advisor to choose.	_____ _____
2. You might not understand what you need to do.	_____ _____
3. You don't understand lectures very well.	_____ _____

Practice 1.2: Talk about your worries

Directions

1. Write down a worry you really have about school, or your life as a student in America, on the chart below.
2. When everyone is ready, stand up and walk around asking different classmates for advice.

Start your conversations like this:

Toshi:	Hey, how's it going, Sami?
Sami:	Oh, alright, I guess. I'm a little worried about (school).
Toshi:	What's up?
Sami:	Well, I'm afraid . . .

3. Take notes on the chart below.
4. When the activity is finished, prepare a one minute presentation for the class. Without reading, talk about what you are worried about and the advice you received.

YOUR WORRY: _____

_____

ADVICE YOU RECEIVED
1.
2.
3.
4.
5.
6.
7.
8.

SECTION 2: CHOOSING A
CLASS TO VISIT

Preview Questions

1. Would it be best to visit a small class or a large class? A class for students in their first year of classes or for students in their final year? Why?

2. How can you learn about the size or level of a class before you visit?

3. How do college students learn where and when classes meet?

4. How can you find out where a professor's office is?

Overview 2

Directions

1. Repeat the phrases after your teacher, making notes about intonation and stress.
2. Find some of these expressions in the Model Conversation on pages 255 and 256 and underline them.
3. Try to think of more expressions to add to the Overview.

Asking about a class to visit

1. What class would you recommend (visiting)?

2. Who is the instructor?

3. What is the (class) like?

4. What level class is it?

5. Where and when does it meet?

6. _____

7. _____

Contacting an instructor

1. I'd like to talk with (Professor Black), is (he/she) in now?

2. Could you tell me when (Professor Black)'s office hours are?

3. Could I leave a message for (Professor Black)?

4. How can I find (the Art department)?

5. _____

6. _____

Practice 2.1: Read a schedule of classes

A. Before you can choose a class to visit, you will need to look at a schedule of classes for the college. Below is one example taken from a college class schedule.

Directions

1. Study the diagram marked "KEY."
2. Look at the timetable of Anthropology classes.

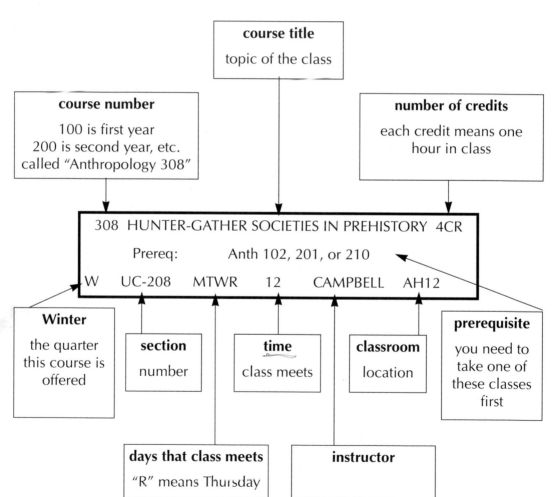

ANTHROPOLOGY

102 INTRODUCTION TO HUMAN ORIGINS 5CR

W	UC-201	MTWRF	10	STEVENSON	BH109

201 INTRODUCTION TO CULTURAL ANTHROPOLOGY 5CR

F	UC 001	MTWRF	8	KIMBALL	AH100
F	UC 002	MTWRF	10	YOUNG	AH100
W	UC-202	MTWRF	12	KIMBALL	AH100
W	UC-202	MTWRF	2	MARSHALL	LH3
S	UC-401	MTWRF	8	LOUCKY	AH4

210 INTRODUCTION TO ARCHAEOLOGY 5CR

F	UC-003	MTWRF	9	CAMPBELL	ES313
S	UC-402	MTWRF	10	CAMPBELL	ES100

215 INTRODUCTORY BIOLOGICAL ANTHROPOLOGY 5CR
Register for a lect and a lab

Lecture(s)

W	UC-204	MWRF	11	STEVENSON	ES80

Lab(s)

W	UC-205	T	8-10	STEVENSON	AH317
W	UC-206	R	8-10	STEVENSON	AH317

301 DEVELOPMENT OF ANTHROPOLOGY 5CR
Prereq: Anth 201.

F	UC-004	MW	2-4:30	LOUCKY	ES313
S	UC-403	MTWRF	11	BOXBERGER	AH102

B. Answer these questions on your own, then check your answers with a partner. Next, take turns asking questions about other classes listed in the schedule above.

1. What is the course number for "Introduction to Human Origins"?

2. What department is it in?

3. Is it a beginning or an advanced course?

4. What days does the class meet?

5. What time does the class meet?

6. Where is the classroom located?

7. What quarter(s) is this course offered?

8. Who teaches the course?

9. What prerequisites are there for "Introduction to Human Origins"?

10. What other courses are offered by the Anthropology department in the Spring?

Practice 2.2: Choosing a class from a local class schedule

> Your teacher will bring in class schedules from a local community college or university. Use this schedule to choose a class which you would like to visit for this unit.

Directions

1. Read the class schedule carefully.
2. Choose three beginning-level classes which interest you.
3. Write all the important information below.
4. Ask your teacher for information you can't find.

1.

Course title:

Department:

Department office:

Course number:

Instructor:

Meeting days and time:

Location:

2.

Course title:

Department:

Department office:

Course number:

Instructor:

Meeting days and time:

Location:

3.

Course title:

Department:

Department office:

Course number:

Instructor:

Meeting days and time:

Location:

Practice 2.3: Locate "your" professor

Directions

Choose one of the classes you investigated in practice 2.2 on page 264. Use the information you have about the class to practice each of the following activities. Your teacher may bring materials that help you find the information you need.

1. Reread the conversation between the secretary and Veronique in the Model Conversation on pages 255 and 256.
2. Take turns with your partner role-playing "the student" and "the secretary," but use the true name of the professor and class you hope to visit. (The "secretary" should create information about office location and office hours that you haven't found yet.)
3. Visit or call the department of the professor whose class you want to visit.
4. Find out the professor's office hours, the office location, and the professor's office phone number.
5. Keep this information. You will use it later in the chapter when you visit that professor's office.

SECTION 3: ASKING PERMISSION TO VISIT A CLASS

Preview Questions

1. Is it permitted to visit a regular class if you are not enrolled in (registered for) that class? How could you find out?

2. How do students know what kind of exams and homework there will be?

3. If you visit a class, when should you arrive? Should you leave early? Should you participate in class? Should you talk to the professor after class?

4. In your home country, have you ever talked to an instructor in his or her office? How did you feel?

5. How do you think relations between American professors and students might be different from such relations in your country?

Overview 3

Directions

1. Repeat the phrases after your teacher, making notes about intonation and stress.
2. Find some of these expressions in the Model Conversation on pages 255 and 256 and underline them.
3. Try to think of more expressions to add to the Overview.

Introducing yourself and your project

1. My name is (Veronique). I'm from (Belgium) and I'm here studying English in (the Intensive English Program).

2. I hope to (become a regular student here, soon).

3. I'd like to visit your class to (see what an American class is like).

4. My homework project is to visit an American college class.

5. _____

6. _____

Asking permission to visit a class

1. I'd like to visit your (East Asian Studies) class because I've heard so much about it from (my roommate). May I visit once this week?

2. I studied (accounting at my university) so I'm very curious to visit your (Accounting 212) class. Would it be O.K. with you if I visited one of your next classes?

3. _____

4. _____

Practice 3.1: Do a class role-play on asking permission to visit a class

Directions

In this practice, you will role-play talking to a professor. Your teacher will assign the following roles.

If you are assigned the role of a student, look at the student directions. If you are assigned the role of a professor, carefully read the directions for professors.

Roles

A. Professor Stevenson, Anthropology Department

B. Professor Miller, Psychology Department

C. Professor Parris, Political Science Department

D. Professor Jackson, History Department

E. A student who wants to visit Psychology 201: Introduction to Psychology (and) Political Science 250: The American Political System

F. A student who wants to visit History 104: American History since 1865 (and) Anthropology 102: Introduction to Human Origins

G. A student who wants to visit History 280: Introduction to East Asian Civilization (and) Anthropology 201: Introduction to Cultural Anthropology

H. A student who wants to visit Psychology 219: Psychology of Sex Roles (and) Political Science 260: Introduction to International Politics

Students look here:

1. Find the professor whose class you wish to visit.

2. Knock at the professor's door.

3. Explain who you are.

4. Explain what you want to do.

5. Explain why you are interested in THAT class.

6. Ask for an extra syllabus.

7. Thank the professor and say goodbye.

Professors look here:

Preparation

1. Put on the name-tag the teacher gives you.

2. Study the list of the classes you teach, marked in a box below.

3. Move to a corner of the room and "set up your office."

4. You will need a sign on your desk with the department name on it.

5. You will need an extra chair for students who come to visit you.

A

Professor Stevenson
Anthropology Department

102 Introduction to Human Origins

201 Introduction to Cultural
Anthropology

B

Professor Miller
Psychology Department

201 Introduction to Psychology

219 Psychology of Sex Roles

C

Professor Parris
Political Science Department

250 The American Political System

260 Introduction to International
Politics

D

Professor Jackson
History Department

104 American History since 1865

280 Introduction to East Asian
Civilization

Activity

1. Greet the student who knocks on your door.

2. Ask the student to sit down.

3. Ask a few questions when the student explains things to you.

4. Give the student permission to visit. Decide what day is good for you.

5. Say goodbye to the student.

REVIEW OF OVERVIEW EXPRESSIONS

Directions

1. Write one word in each of the blanks in the following conversation.
2. After you fill in all the blanks, compare your answers with those of a classmate.
3. Together, compare your answers with those in the Overviews on pages 257, 261, and 266.
4. Read the conversation together.

Wu-Mei: What's up Carlos?

Carlos: I'm **1.** _____ about starting regular classes in the fall. I'm **2.** _____ I **3.** _____ not be able to follow the lectures.

Wu-Mei: I know how you feel, but don't worry. If I **4.** _____ you I **5.** _____ visit some classes now.

Carlos: What class would you **6.** _____ visiting?

Wu-Mei: How about my Econ class?

Carlos: What **7.** _____ class is it?

Wu-Mei: It's an introductory-level class; Econ 101.

Carlos: When does it **8.** _____ ?

Wu-Mei: On Tuesdays and Thursdays from 10 to 12.

Carlos: **9.** _____ is the instructor, anyway?

Wu-Mei: Her name is Dr. Campbell.

Carlos: What is she **10.** _____ ?

Wu-Mei: She was really friendly when I stopped by her office.

Carlos: **11.** _____ can I find her office?

Wu-Mei: She's in the Humanities building on the second floor.

Carlos: Do you know **12.** _____ her office hours **13.** _____ ?

Wu-Mei: Every day at 12:00, I think.

Carlos: O.K. Thanks for all your help!

Wu-Mei: Sure. Let me know what she says.

(Carlos goes to Professor Campbell's office hour.)

Carlos: Hello Professor Campbell. My name is Carlos.

Professor: Nice to meet you, Carlos. What can I do for you?

Carlos: Would it **14.** _____ O.K. **15.** _____ you if I **16.** _____ one of your Econ 101 lectures?

Professor: That would fine. Why are you interested in visiting?

Carlos: I'd **17.** _____ to visit your class to see what a college class is like. I'm here **18.** _____ English, and I've **19.** _____ so much **20.** _____ your Econ class from my friend Wu-Mei.

Professor: Well, you're welcome to come anytime.

Activity 1: Talk with a professor

> Professors have busy schedules. If you have difficulty meeting the professor to ask permission, or to thank him or her, try leaving a phone message or a written note.

A. Role-play your visit

Directions

With a partner, role-play visiting the professor whose class you have chosen to visit. Use the information you collected in Practice 2.2 on page 264 and 2.3 on page 265 to use real names and class information in your role-play. Remember to:

_____ use a correct greeting

_____ introduce yourself clearly

_____ explain your project, or experience, clearly

_____ speak naturally (without reading)

_____ use correct language (grammar)

_____ ask permission or give thanks politely

_____ close the message, repeating any important information

B. Record a message to your teacher

1. Record two messages on an audiocassette, or on a telephone answering machine if your teacher requests. Imagine your messages will be heard by the professor whose class you hope to visit.

    a. In the first message, ask permission to visit the class.

    b. In the second, thank the professor after your visit.

2. Use the checklist in part A as you prepare your recordings.

3. With a partner in class, role-play having the professor return your call and the conversation you might have.

C. Write practice messages

Practice writing notes that you could leave for a professor whose class you would like to visit.

1. Write one note to ask permission.
2. Write a second note to thank the professor after you have visited.
3. Look at the checklist in part A as your prepare your written messages.

D. Ask permission to visit the class

Visit the professor during his or her office hours and ask permission to visit the class. Be prepared to talk about this experience with your classmates.

Activity 2: Visit a college class

Directions

When you have received permission to visit a class, attend the class one time.

1. Interview a student in the class using the questions in section A, page 323, Appendix 2.
2. During the class, try to take notes on a separate piece or paper.
3. After class, answer the questions in sections B and C on page 324, Appendix 2.
4. Turn in the pages from the Appendix and the notes you took during you class visit.

Activity 3: Report back about your experience

Directions

With one or two partners, discuss your class visit.

1. Describe the class and classroom.
2. Describe what happened in class that day.
3. Describe what topic was presented or discussed.
4. Compare the class you visited with classes in your home country.
5. Describe the student you interviewed.
6. Share any interesting information you learned from the interview.
7. Describe how you felt during this experience.

Activity 4: Interview an international student enrolled in college classes

Directions

> International students already enrolled in college classes can be a tremendous resource for you as you prepare to enter college classes yourself. Take advantage of their experience, and ask their advice.

Interview an international student enrolled in college classes. Ask the questions listed in the interview on page 327 of Appendix 2. Add any other questions you would like to ask. Prepare to report on what you learned to the rest of the class.

Activity 5: Keep an oral journal

Directions

On an audiocassette, explain to your teacher about one of the interviews you did in this chapter. Remember to do the following:

_____ introduce the person you interviewed

_____ speak naturally, without reading

_____ tell about something interesting you learned

_____ tell about something you would like to learn more about

_____ speak for 3 to 5 minutes

Activity 6: Evaluate your work

Do you feel confident about being a student in a regular college class? Answer the following questions, then review the advice given below.

1. Can you use a timetable to find out about classes and instructors?

    Yes   So-so   No

2. Were you relaxed when talking to the college instructor?

    Yes   So-so   No

3. Do you feel comfortable in a regular college classroom?

    Yes   So-so   No

4. Could you understand what the professor said?

    Yes   So-so   No

5. Could you take notes during the lecture?

    Yes   So-so   No

6. Do you know what kind of exams or projects are common in regular college classes?

    Yes   So-so   No

Did you answer "No" to any of the questions? You should talk to your teacher or another international student for advice on how to prepare this skill. Don't worry. With practice you will gain confidence.

Did you answer "So-so" to any of the questions? Try to think of ways you can improve your confidence in this area. What could you practice? What advice could you ask for from your teacher or students already attending regular classes?

Did you answer "Yes" to any of the questions? Congratulations! You have one of the skills you will need to succeed in a regular college classroom. Encourage others who may still be unsure.

CHAPTER TWELVE

PREPARING FOR FUTURE CHALLENGES

In this chapter, you will prepare to start taking college classes. You will learn how to:

- talk about your plans for the future
- state your concerns
- locate school support systems
- ask for help
- manage your time
- take lecture notes
- study for tests

· ·

In this chant you will practice some vocabulary and expressions you can use to talk about time management.

📼 Directions

1. Listen to the chant.
2. Repeat after your teacher.
3. Practice the chant several times with a partner. One of you reads A, the other reads B.

    A: THINGS are GETting SERious,
        NO more TIME to PLAY,
        I'd LOVE to go out DANCing,
        but I've GOT a TEST toDAY.

        B: COME on, COME on,
            the STARS are SHINing.
            COME on, COME on,
            DANCE with ME.

    A: You KNOW I'd LOVE to GO,
        but CAN'T we MAKE it LATer?
        I'd BE OUT on the DANCE FLOOR,
        but I've GOT to WRITE this PAPer.

        B: COME on, COME on,
            the MOON is FULL.
            COME on, COME on,
            DANCE with ME.

MODEL CONVERSATION 1

Directions

1. Read the conversation silently.
2. Listen to the model conversation.
3. Read it out loud twice with a classmate, changing roles each time.
4. Answer the questions that follow.

(Nita has just started her first quarter at college. A student in her Sociology class has been hired by the school to tutor Nita for two hours a week. The student is someone who is doing very well in the class and who is trained to tutor other people. This is Nita's first meeting with the tutor.)

Erin: It's nice to meet you, Nita. Are you just here as an exchange student?

Nita: No, I'm planning to get my two-year degree here and then transfer to a four-year college.

Erin: Have you decided on a major yet?

Nita: Not yet. I'm just working on my general requirements right now.

Erin: What would you like to do in the future?

Nita: I don't know. I want to do something to help the environment, you know, recycling or something like that.

Erin: Neat! Well, Joe said you needed some tutoring.

Nita: I'm having trouble with Sociology this term. I was hoping you could help me do better on the tests.

Erin: Well, why don't you show me the test you just got back.

(Erin looks at the test paper.)

Nita: What do you think of my answers? Are they clear?

Erin: Well, I think I understand what you're trying to get at here about gender roles, but you mixed up the definitions of cultural relativity and ethnocentrism.

Nita: I know, there were just so many words to remember!

Erin: Do you write out the definitions of the words and study them before the test?

Nita: No, but I underline them and reread them in the text.

Erin:	I think it would help if you rewrite them yourself on flashcards and drill yourself before the exam. Why didn't you answer question number three?
Nita:	I ran out of time.
Erin:	You should always answer every question, even if all you write are the key ideas, or a list. At least you can get partial credit.
Nita:	How can I tell which questions are going to be on the test? I don't know what to expect.
Erin:	You need to make up questions that you think the teacher might ask based on the text and your lecture notes, and then answer them in writing before the test. Let's try making some questions together right now.

Questions on Model Conversation 1:

1. What expressions does Nita use to talk about her future goals?
2. How does Nita ask Erin for help?
3. What trouble does Nita seem to be having with Sociology?
4. What expressions does Erin use to give Nita advice?

SECTION 1: GETTING HELP FROM SCHOOL STAFF

Preview Questions

1. Why is it better to have a clear goal rather than a vague goal for your future study plans?

2. Do you set aside regular times to study? Why or why not?

3. Where do you usually study? Can you concentrate well there? Why or why not?

4. Is there anyone at your school who can help you improve your study habits? If so, what is the person's title? Where is that office?

Overview 1

Directions

1. Repeat the phrases after your teacher, making notes about intonation and stress.
2. Find some of these expressions in Model Conversation 1 on pages 277 and 278 and underline them.
3. Try to think of more expressions to add to the Overview.

Talking about your goals

1. I'm hoping to (attend the university this Fall).

2. I'm planning on (doing an internship with a business).

3. I'm thinking about (majoring in electrical engineering).

4. I intend to (be here again next year).

5. _____

6. _____

Stating concerns

1. I'm having trouble with (spelling).

2. I'm worried about (keeping up with the workload).

3. I'm not sure about (how you wanted us to answer question #2).

4. I'm having a problem with (Chapter 10).

5. _____

6. _____

Asking for help

1. I was hoping you could tell me how I can (improve my chances of getting into the Environmental Studies Department).

2. I was wondering if you could (give me some advice).

3. What do you think of (the conclusion)? Is it clear?

4. What can I do to (improve this part)?

5. _____

6. _____

Giving advice

1. Maybe you should (add more detail about why you think that way).

2. Have you thought of (finishing up your Associate of Arts degree before you try to transfer)?

3. I think it would help if (you see a career counselor at school).

4. You need to (go to school part-time until your English gets stronger).

5. _____

6. _____

Clarifying advice

1. What if (I just ask my friend to tutor me)?

2. How can I tell (if I need a letter of recommendation)?

3. What do I need to do (if I want to get into medical school)?

4. (How many credits) do I have to (take to be full-time)?

5. _____

6. _____

Practice 1.1: Role-play asking for help

Direction

A. With a partner, think of and write down a problem or concern each of the following college personnel could help you with.

1. an academic and/or admissions advisor

2. a psychological counselor

3. an international student advisor

4. an international student activities coordinator

5. a peer tutor

B. Take turns role-playing a student and a college staff member with your partner. Use expressions from the Overview on pages 279 and 280.

The student:

- introduces himself or herself and tells about his or her goals
- states his or her concerns
- asks for help about the concern
- clarifies the staff member's advice

The college staff member:

- asks questions about the student's goals and concerns
- gives advice

Practice 1.2: Identify and change poor study habits

Directions

A. 1. Read the following conversation with a partner.
   2. Make a list of Nita's poor study habits.
   3. Put a check next to each bad habit you share with Nita.

(Nita is visiting Joe, her advisor, in his office.)

Joe: Why do you think you're having trouble?

Nita: I just never seem to have enough time. The English is really hard for me, and it takes me twice as long to read the textbook or do the homework as everyone else.

Joe: Tell me a little bit about how you study. How many hours a day would you say you study now?

Nita: Probably about one or two on weekdays, and two or three hours a day on the weekends.

Joe: What time of day do you usually study?

Nita: From about eleven at night.

Joe: Why so late?

Nita:	I like to practice English conversation with my roommates in the evening after dinner.
Joe:	Can't you study during the day?
Nita:	I have a couple of hours between classes, but that's the time I see other Iranian friends.
Joe:	Where do you usually study?
Nita:	In my room at home.
Joe:	Do you have a desk?
Nita:	No, I lie on the bed.
Joe:	Why don't you study in the library?
Nita:	At home I can relax, listen to music, and eat while I study.
Joe:	Do you have a study schedule?
Nita:	What do you mean?
Joe:	Do you write down the things you need to do and the times you will do them every day and every week?
Nita:	No, I hate doing that. It just makes me feel more stressed out.
Joe:	I see. Well, thanks for answering my questions. I think I've got some ideas for things you could try.

B. With your partner:

1. Decide what advice Joe should give Nita.
2. Write out an ending to the conversation in which Joe gives advice to Nita. Use expressions from Overview 1 on pages 279 and 280.
3. Read your ending out loud to the class.

C. 1. For one week, follow the advice that you made Joe give Nita.
   2. Report on your progress in your oral journal (see Activity 3, page 296).

Practice 1.3: Identify goals and manage your time

Directions

A. 1. Fill out the "Time Management Self-Assessment Questionnaire" below.
   2. Work in pairs to interview and give each other feedback using the form on page 328, Appendix 2. Use expressions from the Overview on page 280 to give and clarify advice.
   3. Based on your partner's feedback, rewrite your answers to your questionnaire on another piece of paper and turn it in to your teacher for comments.

Time Management Self-Assessment Questionnaire

1. What are some of your long-term goals?

2. What are some of your short-term goals?

3. What skills or information do you need to help you reach your goals?

4. What obstacles stand in your way?

5. How can you solve these problems? Where can you go for help?

6. Do you usually plan how you will spend your day? Do you have a daily or weekly schedule? Why or why not?

7. At the beginning of the school term, do you write down due dates of major assignments? Do you schedule time for working on different assignments? Why or why not?

8. What do you need to change in order to manage your time better?

B. Fill out the Daily Planner on page 329, Appendix 2 for tomorrow.

1. List all the things you have to do tomorrow, including any meetings, assignments, errands, or things you need to bring.
2. Look back at your goals from your Self-Assessment Questionnaire. Try to include something in your plan for tomorrow that is connected to your short- or long-term goals.
3. Put a star next to the most important items.
4. Carry your daily planner with you tomorrow and cross off things as you do them. (You do not need to complete everything—you can add the things you didn't do to a planner for the next day.)
5. Create and use your own daily planner or "to do" list every day for one week. At the end of the week, fill out the self-evaluation form in Appendix 2, page 330, and hand it in to your teacher.
6. Report on your use of a daily planner in your next oral journal (see Activity 3, page 296).

C. Fill out the Weekly Planner on pages 331 and 332 of Appendix 2 for the next week.

1. Be sure to include all your regular activities such as classes, work, meals, leisure activities, and the times you plan to wake up and go to bed.
2. Also include any assignments or tests that you know about. Be sure to schedule time for each class separately.
3. Check your weekly planner every day next week, and add anything new or anything that you forgot.
4. After one week, exchange planners with a partner and give each other feedback using the form on page 333 of Appendix 2. Then turn the form in to your teachers.

MODEL CONVERSATION 2

● ●

Directions

1. Read the conversation silently.
2. Listen to the model conversation.
3. Read it out loud twice with a classmate, changing roles each time.
4. Answer the questions that follow.

> *(Chris and Nita are in the same Sociology class. Chris runs into Nita in the school lounge. Nita is trying to study for Sociology.)*

Chris: Hi, Nita, how'd you do on that test last week in Sociology?

Nita: I bombed it!

Chris: Really? What'd you get?

Nita: A 63.

Chris: Oh, that's not so bad. The class average was only 75 or something. His tests are really tough. Don't let it get you down!

Nita: Yeah, well, my main problem is the English. You know, there're so many new words—I have to learn all that terminology plus the Sociology!

Chris: Listen, you're not the only one. It's like a foreign language to me, too.

Nita: Seriously, though, Chris, I could really use somebody to study with. Why don't we get together and quiz each other on this stuff sometimes?

Chris: Sure, Nita. I could use the review.

Nita: Well . . . do you have a minute right now? Could you quiz me on these definitions?

Chris: Yeah, I guess so. (*sits down*) Let me look at these. Oh, you made some flashcards. Do you want me to quiz you on the term or the definition?

Nita:	Maybe the words first.
Chris:	Okay. It's a word that means, "Everything that is learned and is transferable."
Nita:	"Culture."
Chris:	You got it. Okay, next. What do we call "special norms"?
Nita:	"Folkways."
Chris:	Close! Those are "casual norms." Try again.
Nita:	I don't know.
Chris:	I'll give you a hint. What's the opposite of "less"?
Nita:	More?
Chris:	Right. "Mores." Mores are like cultural or group rules.
Nita:	Oh, I get it. Okay. Next!

Questions on Model Conversation 2:

1. How does Nita ask Chris to study with her?
2. How does Chris accept the invitation?
3. How does Chris ask how she can help quiz Nita?
4. What are some expressions Chris uses to prompt or give hints to Nita?

SECTION 2: STUDYING WITH A CLASSMATE

● ●

Preview Questions

1. What techniques do you use for memorizing new words and information?
2. What are some good ways to study for tests?
3. What are the advantages and disadvantages of studying with a friend?

Overview 2

Directions

1. Repeat the phrases after your teacher, making notes about intonation and stress.
2. Find some of these expressions in Model Conversation 2 on pages 285 and 286 and underline them.
3. Try to think of more expressions to add to the Overview.

Asking a classmate to study with you

1. I could really use somebody to study with.
2. Do you want to get together and (study for the test)?
3. Do you have a minute (right now)?
4. Why don't we (get together and quiz each other)?
5. _____
6. _____

Accepting an invitation to study together

1. Sure, I could use (the review).
2. That'd be great. When do you want to get together?
3. That'd help me, too.
4. Okay, let's try it.
5. _____
6. _____

Asking how you can help the other person

1. Do you want me to (quiz you on the term or the definition)?
2. How do you want me (to quiz you)?
3. Shall I (ask you questions about the textbook)?
4. Which would be better, (to just tell you the answer or to give you hints)?
5. _____
6. _____

Prompting/Giving hints

1. It's a word that means . . .
2. Close. I'll give you a hint.
3. It sounds like (the opposite of "less").
4. It starts with (an M).
5. _____
6. _____

Practice 2.1: Memorize vocabulary using flashcards

Directions

Use expressions from Overview 2 on pages 285 and 286 to do the following tasks.

1. Ask a classmate to study with you. Sit down together.
2. Make flashcards for one of the lists below. Write the word on one side of the card and the definition on the other. Make the definitions yourself by looking at how they are used later in this chapter, looking them up in the dictionary, or asking your teacher.
3. Take turns quizzing each other using the flashcards. Read each word and ask for the definition. Then read each definition and ask for the word.

Example

A: **What does** "assess" **mean?**

B: "Grade someone."

A: **Close. I'll give you a hint:** you should do it to your goals every week.

B: **Does it mean,** "to evaluate"?

A: **That's right! It means,** "to evaluate or judge something critically for the purpose of taking action."

List 1: words/definitions

1. avoid = try to not do something

2. assess

3. procrastinate

4. obstacle

5. overwhelming

6. prioritize

List 2: words/definitions

1. chunk = piece, block, bit

2. socialize

3. motivation

4. deadline

5. distraction

6. cram

Practice 2.2: Take and review lecture notes

Directions

A. 1. Read through the notes in Figure 12.1, page 290.
    2. Listen to your teacher read the first part of the lecture they are based on.
    3. Compare the notes to the script of the lecture, "Time Management and Test Preparation," in Appendix 1, pages 307.
    4. Answer the questions on the next page regarding the lecture notes.

1. What is the lefthand column for? What is the righthand column for? Which column is larger?

2. When did the student write down the "key" words? (Before, during, or after the lecture?) How did he or she choose these "key words"? How can you use the two columns to review your notes and/or study for a test?

3. Did the student write down every word? Which words are missing?

4. What abbreviations did the student use? Can you think of any other common abbreviations?

5. Experts say you should review your lecture notes frequently, not just right before a test. Why is this helpful?

7. What can you do if you don't understand or can't catch something in a lecture?

8. Students who create their own test questions and answer them before tests tend to do much better on the test. Why does this work?

Figure 12.1 Lecture Notes on "Time Management and Test Preparation" Part 1

Key words	Classroom Notes
prepare early	1. people learn best in small chunks not by cramg @ last min.,
	2. sched time thruout quarter to review notes, cards (2-3 x wk, & b4 tests)
how to study	involve as many senses as poss. (sight, sound, etc.)
	1. make up sample q's, put q on 1 side, ans. on back, say both qs & as out loud
	2. rewrite & summarize notes from class, text
	3. make study group (only serious people!)
good habits	1. do hw on time
	2. ask q's if don't understand
	3. eat properly, gd night's sleep, get to class early
	4. day of test, don't sit near friends
obstacles	1. habit of last-min studying (procrastinating)
	2. don't like plannng/sched
	3. use pressure to motivate yrself (lack of other motiv.)
	4. used to being supervised, no habit of studyg on own
	5. can't say no to friends
	6. lack study skills

B. 1. On another piece of paper, make two columns as in Figure 12.1.
   2. Close your book and listen to your instructor read Part 2 of the lecture.
   3. Take notes in the righthand column. Use abbreviations and symbols whenever you can.
   4. After the lecture, rewrite your notes to be clearer and more complete. Write key words or topics in the lefthand column.
   5. Then open your books and compare your notes to the ones in Figure 12.2 below, and to the lecture script on page 308, Appendix 1.

Figure 12.2 Lecture notes on "Time Management and Test Preparation" Part 2

solutions for problems	1. overwhelmed (too much to do); solution = break work into small pieces, decide which are most imp. & order, make sched. for ea. day & ea. wk (usually on Sun.), make daily "to do" list in morn., make sure imp. goals are inc.
	2. unpleasant; solution = identify why don't like something- clarify your goals- think about why you need to do it
	3. avoidance, using escape routes (music, watching TV, movies, socializg, sleepg, eating, sports, getg sick) = go to library- white walls, no distractions
	4. lack of motiv = be yr own manager, develop voice in head, do things 4 yrslf, not other people, make agreements w/people, show them your plans, sched., identify what yr afraid of
summary	1. make sure goals are really imp.- if it's not really your goal, you can't achieve it
	2. be an adult, adults meet deadlines, make choices
	3. enjoy yr life, realize nobody is born with study skills, everyone has to & can learn them

Use expressions from Overview 2 on pages 287 and 288 to do the following tasks.

C. 1. Find a partner. Try to predict what kind of questions might be on a quiz about the "Time Management and Test Preparation" lecture notes.
  2. Write at least ten questions and answers. One question is provided as an example.
  3. Make flashcards with the question on one side and the answer on the other.
  4. Quiz each other orally on both the question and the answer. (Read the answer out loud, and try to tell your partner the question. Read the question out loud, and try to tell your partner the answer.)

Probable test question	Answers
1. How do people learn best?	1. If they study a little bit at a time rather than cramming. Schedule regular times to study, and preview and review class materials at least two or three times a week during the quarter, then again before a test 2. Use several different senses, such as sight (reading), sound (saying answers out loud), and movement (writing) 3. Keep in good physical condition.

D. With a partner or in a group, quiz each other again on vocabulary and concepts using the flashcards you prepared.

E. Take the test on time management and test preparation on pages 334, Appendix 2.*

*Teachers: See Appendix 1, pages 309 and 310 for sample answers.

Activity 1: Listen to a lecture on how to take lecture notes

Directions

1. Prepare two columns in your notebook, a narrow left column and a wide right column. Take notes in the righthand column on your teacher's lecture entitled, "Taking Lecture Notes."* Remember to:

    _____ use abbreviations and symbols

    _____ write down only important words

    _____ number each main point

2. After the lecture, review and edit your notes, rewriting them if necessary. Write down key words in the lefthand column. Find out any information you are missing or don't understand.
3. Work with a partner. Use your notes to create flashcards on vocabulary and test questions. Quiz each other.
4. Take the test on "Taking Lecture Notes" on pages 336 and 337, Appendix 2.**

*Teachers: See Appendix 1, pages 311 and 312 for lecture script.
**Teachers: See Appendix 1, pages 312 and 313 for sample answers.

Activity 2: Inquire about student services

Directions

A. Below is a list of student support services usually found on college campuses. Your teacher will assign one of these services to you. Try to obtain the following information about the service you are assigned:

    a.   location

    b.   phone number

    c.   contact person (name and title)

STUDENT SUPPORT SERVICES
1. Admissions advising
2. Registration advising
3. Math and English placement testing
4. International student advising
5. Classes in ESL for students already taking regular classes
6. Tutoring
7. Study skills instruction
8. Academic counseling
9. Career counseling
10. Psychological counseling
11. Housing assistance
12. Student clubs and activities
13. Other:

B. 1. Make an appointment to interview a staff member about the student service you are assigned. (See Chapter Eight, "Conducting a Successful Interview," on pages 175, 176, 179, and 180 for useful expressions.)
   2. Prepare a list of questions on another piece of paper to ask during your interview. Below are some examples.

Sample questions for the director of a college job center

1. What hours and days is it open?
2. Who are the staff members?
3. Do you need an appointment to see a staff member?
4. What does the Career Resource Center staff help students with?
5. What resources does the Center have for student use?
6. What kind of advice does the Center provide students who are looking for work?
7. Is there any fee for using the Center?
8. Are international students welcome to use the Center?
9. Is there anyone at the Center who is specially trained in helping international students?

---

   3. Tape record your interview or take good notes.
   4. Ask for reference materials from the person you interview to help you prepare a presentation for the class.

C. Give a presentation.

Give a short presentation with one or two other students about your interview. Try to divide the time equally with your partner(s). While you are listening to your classmates' presentations, take notes on another piece of paper.

Activity 3: Keep an oral journal

Directions

In your oral journal, report on the results of:

1. Practice 1.2 page 282, "Changing your poor study habits."
   Be sure to mention:

   _____ which poor study habits you had

   _____ how you tried to change them

   _____ what worked, what didn't work, and why

2. Practice 1.3, Part B, page 284, "Daily Planner,"
   Tell:

   _____ if using a Daily Planner helped you accomplish more

   _____ any problems you had using your Daily Planner

Activity 4: Find out about academic policies and procedures

Directions

A. Look at the catalog of a college you are interested in or are assigned.
   Locate and write down the following information on another piece of
   paper. (Decide with your teacher whether to look for general
   undergraduate, graduate, or specific departmental requirements.)

   1. the international student tuition

   2. the entrance requirements for international students, including the required
      level of English proficiency and how it is measured

   3. the institution's minimum grade point average required for international
      students, and what happens to students who fall below the average

   4. support services available to international students

B. Ask your classmates about the policies and services at the schools they researched. Fill in the blanks in the chart below with their answers. When you finish, discuss which schools appeal to you the most and why.

school name/ tuition	admission reqs/ English scores	minimum GPA/ consequences	support services
①			
②			
③			
④			
⑤			

Activity 5: Evaluate your work

Think back over everything you have learned in this textbook. Now that you have finished, how much do you remember? How much can you use? Circle a number to evaluate your confidence in doing each of the following:

Chapter/Skills	Weak				Strong
1. introducing yourself/ getting to know your classmates	1	2	3	4	5
2. actively learning vocabulary	1	2	3	4	5
3. negotiating with instructors	1	2	3	4	5
4. planning and performing a role-play	1	2	3	4	5
5. giving a speech	1	2	3	4	5
6. discussing your opinion	1	2	3	4	5
7. conducting an interview	1	2	3	4	5
8. debating	1	2	3	4	5
9. getting help at the library	1	2	3	4	5
10. asking for help, using study skills	1	2	3	4	5

If you circled 1 or 2 for any of these skills, talk to your teacher about how you can keep improving your ability in the future. Good luck!

APPENDIX ONE

Chapter 2, Activity 3, pages 39–40: Script for proverbs

Birds of a feather flock together.	People who are similar to each other often stay together in a group.	flock together: get together of a feather: the same kind
Too many cooks spoil the broth.	It's hard to do something when there are too many leaders.	spoil: make bad broth: clear soup
Where there's a will, there's a way.	You can do anything if you really decide it is important.	will: desire way: method
When in Rome do as the Romans do.	Try to get along with other people by doing the same as they do.	
All that glitters is not gold.	The true nature of things may be different from what you see.	glitters: shines
A stitch in time saves nine.	Fix things before they get worse.	stitch: sew
Blood is thicker than water.	People care more about family than about others.	thicker: stronger heavier
Don't make a mountain out of a molehill.	Don't act like a little problem is a big one.	molehill: small hill made by a digging animal
The early bird catches the worm.	You have to move quickly to get what you want.	worm: long, slimy insect that lives in the ground
Beggars can't be choosers.	Don't complain about something you got for free.	beggars: people who ask for money on the street
Two heads are better than one.	You can think of better ideas if you work with another person.	
It's a dog-eat-dog world.	The world is very competitive.	dog-eat-dog: competitive, fighting like two dogs
Every cloud has a silver lining.	Even when something bad happens, a good thing is hidden inside.	silver: valuable lining: inside

"PLEASE BE QUIET"

"YOU DROPPED YOUR WALLET"

"DO YOU KNOW THE TIME?"

"PLEASE FOLLOW ME"

"PLEASE HAVE SOME TEA"

"I'M SO HUNGRY"

"IT REALLY LOOKS LIKE RAIN TODAY"

"YOU LOOK REALLY NICE TODAY"

"WATCH OUT!"

"YOU'RE CRAZY"

"WOULD YOU LIKE A RIDE?"

"PLEASE DON'T SHOOT!"

"THAT'S THE FUNNIEST THING I'VE EVER SEEN!"

(IN AN ELEVATOR) "ARE YOU GOING DOWN?

"COULD YOU PUT OUT THAT CIGARETTE?"

"HOW MUCH DID THAT COST?"

"COULD YOU HELP ME PUSH MY CAR?"

"WHERE IS THE POST OFFICE?"

"I'M REALLY SORRY TO HEAR THAT"

Chapter 5, Practice 3.1, page 111: Script for teacher's demonstration

GETTING A TOLL-FREE NUMBER

Teacher: Today I'd like to teach you how to find and use toll-free telephone numbers. Toll-free means that you don't have to pay for the call. I chose this topic because we all want to have lower phone bills.

First, dial 1–800–555–1212. Make sure to dial a "1" first. Next the operator will say, "800 directory, how can I help you?"

After that, you should say the name of the business you want to call.

Next, the operator will give you the 800 number, if there is one listed. "Listed" or "listing" means that the operator can find it in her book.

Finally, you say thanks, hang up, and try calling that number. It won't cost you anything to call.

Is that pretty clear, or should I explain again?

Classmate: Is there always a free number?

Teacher: Not always, but it's worth a try. Any other questions? (*pause*) O.K., I think you're ready to try it now.

Why don't you try it? (*chooses a classmate*) You pretend to call the 800 directory because you want the number of the Hilton hotel in San Francisco, O.K.? I'll be the operator.

Classmate: O.K. Uhm. (*pretends to dial*) 1–800–555–1212.

Teacher: Ring-a-ling-a-ling. 800 directory, this is Ann.

Classmate: Uhm. Uhm. I'd like . . . oh, I forget!

Teacher: You're doing fine. You've almost got it. Say, "I'd like the number of the Hilton hotel in San Francisco, please."

Classmate: I'd like the number of the Hilton hotel in San Francisco, please.

Teacher: One moment. I don't show a listing for the Hilton in San Francisco, but I do show a general reservations number.

Classmate: Thank you.

Teacher: (*with a machine-like voice*) The toll-free number is 800–445–8667. Repeat. 800–445–8667. If you have further questions a directory assistance operator will come back on the line momentarily.

(*The role-play ends.*)

Teacher: That was great! You've got it! Does anyone else want to try? (*pause*) Thanks for being such a good audience, and I hope your phone bills will be a little lower now!

Chapter 8, Practice 1.2, page 177

CARDS FOR MEMBERS OF GROUP A

TOPIC 1: Marriage customs, for Anthropology class

When someone agrees to be your partner, ask and discuss the following question:

1.   How do people in your culture find someone to marry?
2.   How are weddings celebrated?

TOPIC 2: Differences between men and women, for Sociology class

When someone agrees to be your partner, do the following interview:

1.   Do you believe men and women think about or feel things differently? Please explain your opinion.
2.   Do you think a woman can be a good boss? Why or why not?

TOPIC 3: Friendships, for an Oral History class

When someone agrees to be your partner, do the following interview:

1.   Tell me about a childhood friend.
2.   What are the important characteristics of a friend?

TOPIC 4: Grandparents, for an Oral History class

When someone agrees to be your partner, do the following interview:

1.   Tell me what you know about your grandparents.
2.   What do old people usually do in your culture? Where do they live?

TOPIC 5: Changes in your culture, for Anthropology class

When someone agrees to be your partner, do the following interview:

1. How is your life the same as or different than your parents' lives?
2. How has life in your country changed in the last 50 years?

TOPIC 6: Your country and its regions, for Geography class.

When someone agrees to be your partner, do the following interview:

1. What regions make up your country? Please describe them.
2. How is the language or customs different in different regions?

TOPIC 7: Finding and changing jobs, for Business class

When someone agrees to be your partner, do the following interview:

1. Please tell me about the jobs members of your family have.
2. How do people usually find jobs?
3. Do people change companies or types of job often?

TOPIC 8: Women in the workforce, for Business class

When someone agrees to be your partner, do the following interview:

1. Do women and men have similar work positions and pay in your country? Has it always been like that?
2. How is child-care provided for working parents?

CARDS FOR MEMBERS OF GROUP B

You will only agree to be interviewed about:

TOPIC 1: MARRIAGE CUSTOMS

You will only agree to be interviewed about:

TOPIC 2: DIFFERENCES BETWEEN MEN AND WOMEN

You will only agree to be interviewed about:

TOPIC 3: FRIENDSHIPS

You will only agree to be interviewed about:

TOPIC 4: GRANDPARENTS

You will only agree to be interviewed about:

TOPIC 5: CHANGES IN YOUR CULTURE

You will only agree to be interviewed about:

TOPIC 6: YOUR COUNTRY AND ITS REGIONS

You will only agree to be interviewed about:

TOPIC 7: FINDING AND CHANGING JOBS

You will only agree to be interviewed about:

TOPIC 8: WOMEN IN THE WORK-FORCE

Chapter 9, Practice 1.1, pages 196–197: Definitions

(An) Abstract:	a short paragraph giving the main ideas in the article
Alphabetical Order:	books or words organized in the order of the alphabet; first words that begin with A, then B, then C, etc.
(An) Article:	a story or report in a magazine, journal, or newspaper
(An) Author:	the person who wrote the article or book
(A) Call Number:	a special number for each book that shows where that book is located in the library
Card Catalog:	drawers of cards that show what books are located where in the library
(To) Check Out:	the process of borrowing a book to take home
(A) Computer Search:	using a computer to find out information on books and articles on a topic
Editorials on File:	a collection of essays from newspapers organized by topic
(An) Encyclopedia:	many volumes of books with general information on many topics, organized alphabetically (A to Z)
(A) Fine:	money you must pay because you did something wrong, such as lose a book or return it late
(An) Index:	a list of topics that also explains where you can find information about each topic
(A) Journal:	A professional magazine on one subject area

(A) Loan Desk:	the front desk of a library, where you check out books
(To) Look Up:	to look for information in a book, card catalog, etc.
(A) Main Menu:	the first screen on a computer, where you choose from a list of things to do
Microfiche:	a small piece of plastic paper with tiny photographed pages on it
Microfilm:	a film copy of a book, magazine, journal, or newspaper, which comes on a roll
(To Be) Overdue:	to be late, to return after the "due date"
(A) Periodical:	a magazine or newspaper that is made on a regular schedule, such as once a week/day/or month.
(To) Print Out:	to get a paper copy of what you see on the computer
Reference Area:	the part of the library for general information and research. Reference books must stay in the library.
(A) Subject/Topic:	what you want to read or study about
(A) Subtopic:	a more specific topic; for the topic "alcohol," a subtopic would be "alcohol abuse in children"
(A) Title:	the name of the book or article
(A) Volume:	When a story, group of magazines, or collection of articles fills more than one book, each book is called a volume and given a number

Chapter 12, Practice 2.2, page 289:

Script of lecture, "Time Management and Test Preparation"

Part 1

The topic of my lecture today is time management and test preparation. Many people study and study but still don't do well in classes. What they don't realize is that how you study is just as important as how much you study.

The best way to study is the way that helps you understand and remember what you learn. The key point here is to prepare early. We know from experiments on memory that people learn best in "small chunks" little by little rather than by cramming just before a test. That's why you should schedule time throughout the quarter to review your notes and flashcards. For example, you should review your notes for one course before and after each lecture, or two or three times a week, and then again before a test. It will only take a few minutes each time and you will be able to place the information in your long-term memory.

Next, think about how you study, and try to involve as many of your senses, such as sight and sound, as possible. Don't just reread the textbook, but think of ways to engage yourself actively in the material. For example, make up flashcards based on the text with a question on one side and the answer on the other. Then quiz yourself, saying both the question and answer out loud. Again, don't just reread your notes, but rewrite them more neatly and correctly, and summarize them. Ask your classmates to work with you in a study group - but be sure to ask only serious people. Study groups have a danger of becoming social times!

Also, try to keep good habits in your personal life so that you are rested and calm before a test. Always do your homework on time so that you can ask questions before a test if you don't understand. Be sure to eat properly and get enough sleep throughout the quarter. And on the day of the test, get to class early, and don't sit near friends who might distract you.

Now you know how to study better. Easy, right? Unfortunately, even when we know how to study we don't always do it. We all have inner obstacles that get in our way. Some common obstacles are habits we get into, such as procrastinating, or studying at the last minute. Also, some of us just hate having to plan or schedule things. We see schedules as part of the adult world we are avoiding. Maybe you don't really want to be in school, and only the pressure of a test finally forces you to study. Or perhaps your parents always supervised your study, and you never developed the habit of studying on your own. Maybe you want to be popular and can't seem to say no when your friends invite you out. Finally, you might just lack the study skills I mentioned earlier.

Part 2

If you have any of these obstacles, and all of us have some of them, you must face them and find solutions for them, or they will continue to get in your way. Let me give you some examples. If you are putting something off because it is too much and you feel overwhelmed, try breaking the work into small pieces. Decide which parts are the most important and list them in order. Make a schedule for each day and each week; a good day to do this might be Sunday. Then make a daily list of things to do in the morning, and make sure your most important goals are included.

If you are putting something off because it is unpleasant, try to identify why you don't like it. At the same time, clarify your own goals - even though you may not like something, it may help you get something else you do like. Is it worth it to you?

If you plan to study but then avoid it, you may be using escape routes such as listening to music, watching TV or movies, socializing, sleeping, eating, playing sports, or even getting sick. One solution for this is to go to the library where these escape routes are not available, where there are white walls and no distractions.

If you are not studying because you just aren't motivated, perhaps you will have to develop a new side of yourself. You can call this your "manager side." It's like a voice in your head that tells you to do things for yourself, and not for other people. At the same time, if you have trouble working alone, make agreements with other people to study, show them your plans and schedule, and talk to them to try to identify what you are afraid of.

In summary, studying involves both skills and also a clear understanding of yourself. If no matter what you do, you can't seem to study, make sure that your goals are really important to you. If a goal is not truly your own, you will not be able to achieve it. If it is your goal, maybe you have to decide you are going to be adult, and that means meeting deadlines and making choices as well as enjoying your life. Finally, you should realize that no matter how you may struggle sometimes, nobody is born with study skills. Everyone has to learn them, and at the same time, anyone can learn them.

Chapter 12, Practice 2.2 D, page 292:

Sample answers to "Time Management and Test Preparation" quiz

A. Vocabulary (4 points each)

Define the following terms briefly (in a few words or sentences).

Example

1. something that overpowers or overcomes you
2. try not to do something
3. to list goals in order of importance or accomplishment
4. something that blocks progress or achievement
5. something that takes your attention away from what you should be doing
6. to pass a pleasant time with friends
7. to have a habit of putting off something you should do
8. to study quickly right before a test
9. bit, piece, part
10. to evaluate or judge something critically for the purpose of taking action

B. Short-answer questions on concepts (10 points each)

Write a few sentences or a paragraph answering each question and giving specific examples.

Example: How do people learn best?

1. Study a little bit at a time over a long period of time rather than cramming. 2. Schedule regular times to study, and preview and review class material at least two or three times a week during the quarter, then again before a test. 3. Use several different senses, such as sight (reading), sound (saying answers out loud), and movement (writing). 4. Keep in good physical condition.

1.   What are some good ways to memorize important definitions and facts?

1. Predict problems that will be on the test, and then answer them based on the lectures and your textbook. 2. Make flashcards and quiz yourself or a classmate on both the problem and the answer. 3. Do all your assignments on time and rewrite and summarize your notes from the lectures and textbook regularly. Then you will have time to ask the instructor questions about anything you don't understand before the test.

2. **What obstacles prevent people from managing their time well or using good study techniques?**

1. Bad habits. For example, procrastinating, only working hard under pressure, not being able to say no to friends, or only studying when someone else, like your parents, is supervising you. 2.Not knowing how to study. 3. Thinking that making plans and keeping to a schedule is too troublesome.

3. **If you feel overwhelmed by homework, what can you do?**

1. Break your homework down into small steps. 2. Decide which steps are most important and the order in which you will do them. 3. Make a weekly schedule and a daily "to do" list that includes your most important tasks. 4. Review and change your "to do" list every morning and your weekly schedule every Sunday.

4. **If you find studying unpleasant or try to avoid it, what can you do?**

1. Ask yourself why you dislike it. 2. Decide if your studies really fit in with your goals. 3. Remove yourself from distractions. One of the best ways to do this is simply to go to the library.

5. **How can you motivate yourself to study without the pressure of a last-minute deadline?**

1. Learn to be your own boss. Develop a voice in your head that tells you to do things. 2. Talk to people about your plans and show them your weekly schedule.

6. **What general advice could you give to someone who is struggling with finding enough time to do schoolwork?**

1. Examine your goals and make sure that you really want them. It's hard to succeed at things you don't really want. 2. Make choices about your life. Realize that part of being an adult is meeting deadlines. 3. Finally, learn and apply new study skills. No one is born with good study skills but anyone can learn them. They can make a big difference in your ability to succeed in school.

Chapter 12, Follow Up Activity 1, page 293:

Script of lecture, "Taking Lecture Notes"

Today I will give you some extra tips about how to take good lecture notes. Although a lot depends on the instructor and your listening comprehension, any one of you can learn to take better notes if you follow my advice.

First of all, you should prepare by reading the textbook before you come to class. Look at your syllabus to find out which pages the instructor will lecture on. Take notes on your textbook and look up new vocabulary ahead of time. You might be completely lost and unable to take notes if all the vocabulary and ideas are new to you.

Second, you should come to class a little early and find a seat near the front of the class. If you are early, you will be able to get your pencil and paper ready and organize your notes ahead of time. If you sit close to the front, you will be able to hear better, see the board better, and watch your instructor more closely for non-verbal clues. Also, you are less likely to doze off or daydream if you are close to the instructor.

Next, take notes using the method we have studied in class. Make two columns and take notes on the right side. Use only one side of the paper. The reason for this is that later, when you review your notes, you can add key words in the lefthand column, and use the blank side of the facing page to summarize your notes and make review questions. Your notes will be instantly organized and it will be easy to find and review information. Also, you can quiz yourself later on your notes by covering up the righthand column and trying to say your notes out loud by just looking at the key words and review questions.

Remember when you take notes to try to write more quickly by using abbreviations, symbols, and writing down only the important points. How do you know what is important? Anything the instructor writes on the board is important and should be copied down. Also listen for transition words, such as "first of all," or "another reason," or words that your instructor emphasizes. For example, your instructor may signal that something is important by speaking more loudly or with emotion, by making a certain gesture or facial expression, or by asking a rhetorical question. Each instructor is a little different; observe your instructor carefully to learn what signals he or she uses.

Finally, be sure to review your notes and rewrite any parts that are hard to read or unclear. If you can't understand or are missing something, ask your teacher or a classmate for help, look in your textbook, or look up the information in the library. You should do this within at least 48 hours of the lecture, before you forget the content.

In summary, the key to taking good lecture notes is to be prepared before class, to be attentive in class, to check to make sure you understood after class, and to ask for help when you need it. In other words, taking good lecture notes does not mean just sitting in class while the teacher talks; you must be active and organized in order to really understand and remember the material.

Answers to Follow Up Activity 1: Quiz on "Taking Lecture Notes" (100 points)

A. Vocabulary (4 points each)

Briefly define and/or give examples of the following terms.

1. an outline of a course

2. to fall into a light sleep

3. to imagine something pleasant

4. a section of space or writing stretching from top to bottom (vertically)

5. a shortened form of a word

6. a sign used as a short way of writing something, for example, "+" means "plus"

7. a word that signals a change from one idea to another

8. a question the speaker asks herself or himself, or which does not need an answer

9. a sign, such as a word or gesture, that gives a message

10. listening and watching carefully

B. Short-answer questions on concepts (10 points each)

Write a few sentences or a paragraph answering each question and giving specific examples.

1. Read the pages in the textbook that relate to the next lecture and take notes on the reading. Look up any vocabulary you don't know.

2. You won't be able to follow the lecture if there are a lot of new words and ideas you don't understand.

3. 1. You can get organized and be ready to take notes at the beginning of the lecture. 2. You can see the board and your instructor better. 3. You won't be as likely to fall asleep or think about other things.

4. Draw a line down your paper to make two columns. Take notes on the right side. Add key words later to the left side. Just use one side of each page. Summarize your notes and write review questions on the blank side of the facing page. One advantage is you can find and review information later more easily. Another advantage is you can use the key words and review questions to quiz yourself.

5. 1. If it's on the board. 2. If the instructor uses a transitional expression, like "another reason." 3. If the instructor uses some special signal or gesture.

6. Get help from your teacher or a classmate, or look it up in your textbook or in the library.

APPENDIX TWO

Chapter 2, Activity 3, part B, page 41: Interview about proverbs

Directions

1. Take notes, or tape record your interview.
2. Use the expressions from the Overviews on pages 26, 27, 30, and 31 to help you understand the explanations you hear.
3. When you finish the interview, ask "Could you teach me any other proverbs?" and write these down in your notes.

You could begin your interview like this:

"Excuse me, could I interview you about the meaning of some proverbs? It's for my homework and will take about 15 minutes. What is the meaning of this proverb, in your opinion . . . "

1. Actions speak louder than words.

2. Rome wasn't built in a day.

3. While the cat's away the mice will play.

4. People who live in glass houses shouldn't throw stones.

5. A bird in the hand is worth two in the bush.

6. Don't put all your eggs in one basket.

7. Don't cross a bridge until you come to it.

8. The grass is always greener on the other side of the fence.

9. You can't teach an old dog new tricks.

10. One man's meat is another man's poison.

11. (Other proverbs you have heard).

Chapter 2, Activity 4, part A, page 43: Interview on health resources

Directions

1. Begin your interview with a phrase like the following: "We've been talking about how to keep healthy when you're under stress. Could I ask you a few questions on that topic?"
2. Use expressions from the Overview on page 30 to help you understand the answers you receive.
3. Take notes.

1. What do you do to stay healthy when you are under a lot of stress?

2. What kind of sports or activities are inexpensive and easy to do?

3. Do you know of any nice places to go for a walk or bike-ride? Where?

4. What do you do when you get sick? What do you know about using the health services here?

Chapter 3, Activity 1 C, page 63: Evaluate your classmates' role-play

Directions

Give your classmates feedback on their role-play performances using the score sheet below. Your instructor may ask you to rate one person or the whole group. Your instructor may also ask you to use this feedback to redo your role-play and perform it again.

Names of student(s) observed: _____

_____

		Needs Work				**Excellent**
1.	Voice: loudness, clearness, expressiveness	1	2	3	4	5
2.	Gestures/eye contact/ facial expression	1	2	3	4	5
3.	Faced the audience	1	2	3	4	5
4.	Delivered lines smoothly	1	2	3	4	5
5.	Extra creativity, such as props, costumes, or interesting story	1	2	3	4	5

Total: _____ out of 25 X 4 = _____ out of 100.

What I enjoyed the most about your role-play: _____

_____

_____

How I think you could improve your role-play: _____

_____

_____

Chapter 4, Activity 3, page 94: Evaluate Yourself

Directions

Evaluate your work in this class using this questionnaire. Bring it to your appointment with your instructor.

	poor				**excellent**
1. preparation for class (including homework)	1	2	3	4	5
2. participation in class (including helping classmates)	1	2	3	4	5
3. attendance/promptness	1	2	3	4	5
4. quizzes/tests	1	2	3	4	5
5. other:	1	2	3	4	5
6. other:	1	2	3	4	5
7. my overall achievement	1	2	3	4	5

8. how I could improve:

Chapter 5, Activity 1, part B, page 114: Feedback Form

Directions

Listen as your partner does a demonstration for you. Circle "yes" if your partner did each task well. Circle "needs work" if your partner did not do this, or needs to practice this more. Give this form to your partner after the demonstration.

PERFORMANCE:

spoke loudly with clear pronunciation	yes	needs work
looked at classmates often	yes	needs work
used gestures/real objects to help demonstrate	yes	needs work
checked for understanding	yes	needs work
included and encouraged participation	yes	needs work

CONTENT:

introduced the topic/explained importance or gave background	yes	needs work
used step-by-step language	yes	needs work
explained new vocabulary	yes	needs work
closed the speech	yes	needs work
spoke for an appropriate length of time	yes	needs work

OTHER COMMENTS:

Chapter 7, Practice 3.3, page 163: Report Form

Directions

If you are the note-taker in a discussion, use your notes to fill out this form after the discussion. Hand it in to your teacher.

In our group we talked about the question,

Some people thought

Some of the reasons they gave were

Other people thought

They said that

We concluded that

Chapter 7, Activity 1 F, page 168: Peer Feedback Form

Directions

1. Watch and listen to one of your classmates as he or she takes part in a discussion.
2. Complete the sentences with examples of your classmate's speech and behavior. If your classmate didn't do something because it was not his/her job (for example, he/she was not the leader), write N/A for "not applicable."
3. Give this form to your classmate after the discussion, and explain your evaluation and comments.

CLASSMATE'S NAME _____

CLASSMATE'S ROLE IN THE GROUP _____

DISCUSSION TOPIC _____

1. started the discussion by saying:
   or doing:

2. presented opinions about:

3. presented information about:

4. asked questions about:

5. clarified _____ 's (classmates' names) opinions

6. agreed with these ideas:

7. disagreed with these ideas:

8. showed he/she was listening by (smiling, nodding, making eye contact, etc.)

9. helped keep group on task by:

10. closed the discussion by saying:

Next time, I think my classmate should do _____

_____ more

and _____ less.

Chapter 10, Practice 1.3, part B, #6, page 222:

Article Summary Form

Name:

Name of the newspaper or magazine:

Date of the issue you read:

Title of the article:

Author of the article:

Pages the article was on:

1. Write down the main topic of the article and some of the important points discussed.

2. Write down three facts or quotations from the article that you might use in your debate. (If you write down a quotation, write down who said it.)

   1.

   2.

   3.

Chapter 10, Practice 1.3, part C, #5, page 222:

Interview Report Form

Name:

Date of interview:

Important information about the person you interviewed:

Question 1: _____

Notes:

Question 2: _____

Notes:

Question 3: _____

Notes:

Question 4: _____

Notes:

Question 5: _____

Notes:

Question 6: _____

Notes:

Chapter 10, Activity 5, part B, page 251:

Debate Summary Form

What was the debate proposition?

What were the "pro" arguments?

What were the "con" arguments?

What was your opinion at the start of the debate?

What was your opinion at the end of the debate?

What did you think was the most convincing argument in the debate?

Chapter 11, Activity 2, page 272: Visiting a college class

Interview, Observation, and Reflection Form

Title of Course:
Instructor's Name:
Day/Time:
Location:

A. Interview

Directions

Before or after class, ask one of the students in the class the questions below.

You can begin like this:

"Would you mind if I asked you a few questions about this class?"

1. What is your major?

2. Why are you taking this class?

3. What kind of work do you have to do for this class?

4. How many hours a week do you have to study?

5. How much reading do you have?

6. What kinds of tests are given? How many tests are given during the quarter?

7. Would you call this a hard class? Why or why not?

8. What is the best class you've taken so far? Why did you like it?

B. Observation
   Look around the classroom during your visit, and prepare to answer the
   following questions:

   1. How many students were in the class?

   2. How long was the class?

   3. How did the instructor start the class?

   4. What did the instructor do? Lecture? Ask the students questions?
       Describe in detail. Use extra paper if necessary.

   5. What were the students doing while the instructor was teaching?

   6. Did any students ask the professor questions? If yes, what did they ask?
       Did they raise their hand before asking?

C. Reflection
   (Use another piece of paper if you need more room to write.)

   1. What was the main topic of the class that day?

   2. What was the most difficult thing for you to understand?

   3. Was it difficult or easy to take notes during the class lecture or discussion?
       Why or why not? (Please attach your notes to this report.)

   4. How does this class compare to classes in your home country?
       Be specific: compare the teachers, the students, the rooms, etc.

Chapter 11, Activity 4, page 273: Interview an international student

Directions

Interview someone who has already begun regular college classes.

1. Could you tell me how you felt when you started regular college classes?

2. What was the most difficult thing for you about the classes? Why?

3. How did you choose which classes to take?

4. What techniques do you use to help you understand the lectures?

5. How do you prepare for the tests?

6. What suggestions do you have for being successful in regular college classes?

7. What would you recommend doing as I prepare for entering college classes?

8. (Your own questions)

Chapter 12, Practice 1.3 A, page 283:
Evaluate your classmate's time management

Directions

Ask your partner the following questions. Feel free to offer your partner advice while you are talking.

1. What did you write for your long-term goals?

   • Why did you choose these?

   • When did you first decide these goals?

   • Which goal is the most important to you? Why?

   • When would you like to achieve each goal?

   • Do you feel that what you are doing now is helping to lead you to your goals? Why or why not?

2. What did you write for your short-term goals?

   • Why did you choose them?

   • How soon would you like to achieve them?

   • Which of them are you working on now?

3. What skills or information do you need to reach your goals?

   • How can you get these skills or information?

   • How are you trying to get these skills or information now?

4. What obstacles stand in your way?

   • Which obstacles can you overcome easily by yourself?

   • Which obstacles do you need help with? How will you get this help?

5. Do you plan your day or week? If no, why not? If yes, how?

6. Do you ever forget about homework? Why or why not?

   • Do you ever rush and do homework at the last minute? Why or why not?

7. What would you like to change about the way you manage your time?

Chapter 12, Practice 1.3 B, page 284: Daily Planner Form

DAILY PLANNER

DATE: _____

TIME	TO DO

Chapter 12, Practice 1.3 B, page 284:

Evaluate your use of a daily planner

Directions

1. Fill this out after you have used a daily planner every day for one week. Put a check mark by each statement that applies to you.

2. If you cannot put a check mark, write down the reason why and how you can solve the problem.

3. Turn this form in to your teacher.

Now that I plan my day,

_____ 1. I accomplish at least two or three of my most important goals for each day.

_____ 2. I leave the house and get places on time.

_____ 3. I remember to bring the things I am supposed to.

_____ 4. I don't forget tests or assignments.

_____ 5. I usually feel rested and relaxed.

Chapter 12, Practice 1.3 C, page 284: Weekly planner

WEEKLY PLANNER

DATE: _____ TO _____

	Mon.	Tues.	Wed.	Thurs.	Fri.	Sat.	Sun.
6 A.M.– **8 A.M.**							
8 A.M. – **10 A.M.**							
10 A.M.– **12 P.M.**							
12 P.M.– **2 P.M.**							

2 P.M.– **4 P.M.**						
4 P.M.– **6 P.M.**						
6 P.M. – **8 P.M.**						
8 P.M.– **10 P.M.**						
10 P.M.– **12 A.M.**						

Chapter 12, Practice 1.3 C, page 284:

Evaluate your classmate's Weekly Planner

Directions
1. Look at your partner's weekly planner and use this form to assess the time he or she scheduled for important activities.
2. Give this form to your partner and explain your answers.
3. If you circled "not enough" for something, help your partner think of a way to add it to his or her schedule.
4. If you circled "too much" for something, help your partner think of a way to cut it down or out.

YOUR TIME FOR:	(circle one)		
	not enough	enough	too much
1. REST			
a. sleep	1	2	3
b. seeing friends	1	2	3
c. being alone	1	2	3
2. EXERCISE	1	2	3
3. EATING	1	2	3
a. breakfast	1	2	3
b. lunch	1	2	3
c. dinner	1	2	3
4. HOBBIES/LEISURE ACTIVITIES (Write down your partner's hobbies or leisure activities.)			
a.	1	2	3
b.	1	2	3
c.	1	2	3
5. STUDYING/HOMEWORK			
a. class: _____	1	2	3
b. class: _____	1	2	3
c. class: _____	1	2	3
d. class: _____	1	2	3
6. OTHER (Write down other regular activities your partner has scheduled)			
a.	1	2	3
b.	1	2	3

Chapter 12, Practice 2.2 E, page 292:

"Time Management and Test Preparation" quiz (100 points)

A. Vocabulary (4 points each)

Define the following terms briefly (in a few words or sentences).

Example: proficiency   *skill or knowledge gained through training and practice*

1. overwhelming

2. avoid

3. prioritize

4. obstacle

5. distraction

6. socialize

7. procrastinate

8. cram

9. chunk

10. assess

B. Short-answer questions on concepts (10 points each)

Write a few sentences or a paragraph answering each question and giving specific examples.

Example: How do people learn best?

1. Study a little bit at a time over a long period of time rather than cramming. 2. Schedule regular times to study, and preview and review class material at least two or three times a week during the quarter, then again before a test. 3. Use several different senses, such as sight (reading), sound (saying answers out loud), and movement (writing). 4. Keep in good physical condition.

1. What are some good ways to memorize important definitions and facts?

2. What obstacles prevent people from managing their time well or using good study techniques?

3. If you feel overwhelmed by homework, what can you do?

4. If you find studying unpleasant or try to avoid it, what can you do?

5. How can you motivate yourself to study without the pressure of a last-minute deadline?

6. What general advice could you give to someone who is struggling with finding enough time to do schoolwork?

Chapter 12, Activity 1, page 293: Quiz on "Taking Lecture Notes" (100 points)

A. Vocabulary (4 points each)

Briefly define and/or give examples of the following terms.

1. syllabus

2. doze off

3. daydream

4. column

5. abbreviation

6. symbol

7. transition word

8. rhetorical question

9. signal

10. attentive

B. Short-answer questions on concepts (10 points each)

Write a few sentences or a paragraph answering each question and giving specific examples.

1. What can you do to prepare before class?

2. Why is it important to prepare?

3. Give three reasons you should sit near the front of the class.

4. Describe the method you have learned for taking notes and give at least two advantages of this method.

5. Explain three ways that you can tell if something in a lecture is important.

6. What can you do if you can't read or understand something in your notes?